are we there yet?

to indignity . . .
and beyond!

emily atack

SEVEN DIALS

First published in Great Britain in 2019 by Seven Dials
This paperback edition published in 2020 by Seven Dials
an imprint of The Orion Publishing Group Ltd
Carmelite House, 50 Victoria Embankment
London EC4Y 0DZ

An Hachette UK Company

1 3 5 7 9 10 8 6 4 2

A CIP catalogue record for this book is
available from the British Library.

ISBN (Paperback) 978 1 8418 8369 4
ISBN (eBook) 978 1 8418 8370 0

Printed and bound in Great Britain by Clays Ltd, Elcograf S.p.A.

MIX
Paper from
responsible sources
FSC® C104740
www.fsc.org

www.orionbooks.co.uk

Contents

For my Uncle, Simon Barnes

Prologue

Hiya. This is weird. I'm sat on the 16.40 train from London Euston to Manchester. That's not the weird part. The weird part is that I'm typing on my own laptop for the first time ever. That is honestly no exaggeration. THE FIRST TIME EVER. I've obviously typed on a computer before as a kid – at school in those shabby little computer rooms that smelt like farts, where it was apparently just the perfect time to flirt with the boy you fancied. Swinging around on your chair and saying things to him like, 'I might get plastic surgery when I'm older', for attention. Or on MSN, or secretly trying to look at minger.com with my mates after school (still feel guilty about that). And there was, of course, Myspace, Bebo, Facebook etc. as I became a teen. But this is genuinely the first time I have ever typed on a laptop that I own. I'm 29, and I thought maybe that was a step I should tick off as an adult. So here we are.

It's Wednesday 16 January 2019, and I can honestly say the last year, and especially the last few months, have been the most interesting, insanely challenging, eye-opening and wonderfully life-changing months of my life. I decided to make some very bold decisions and changes, both in my personal wellbeing and in my career. Both of which, over the years, have been at times utterly joyous, and at other times really, REALLY shite. Whose twenties aren't sometimes? But by 2018, I had got to a point where things were at a bit of a standstill and I felt unhappy. Don't get me wrong – I have been blessed with a great life and so many wonderful things have happened to me that I will be forever grateful for. But … I have also found that some of life's struggles have really got the better of me at times. And as the last year of my twenties was creeping closer, I decided to try to take control of my life, whatever that means.

This book is part of that. I'm trying to understand myself more, to work out what I want and to accept that I'm an all right human being, really, just how I am. Doing that properly means looking back and reflecting on how I got to this point: all the highs, the lows, the hangovers, the relationships, the lucky breaks – and breaks I worked my arse off for – that have got me to the here and now. Standing on this exciting but sometimes-bloody-scary precipice of 30, working out how I feel about it and which road I want to go down now. Basically, I hope you're sitting comfortably because you're all my therapists for the next couple of hundred pages. Think of me as that drunk friend who is waffling on in the back of the cab while you scoff your kebab at the end of the long night.

Some of you might know who I am from *The Inbetweeners*, some of you might only know about me from *I'm a Celeb* ..., some of you might have watched me in both. A very small (and I mean a teeny tiny amount of you) may have caught me in the odd film or two, on a random channel, on a Sunday night, when you should probably be asleep and there was nothing else on. But none of you will really know the blurry bits and bumpy moments in between. So, I guess this is a book that fills in those blanks. If you're on the tube to work, I hope you have a nice day. If you're in your bedroom, well done for not being on your phone! Light a scented candle, pretend you're an Instagram influencer (probably take a photo to show off) and get cosy.

are we there yet?

I've got my packet of crisps, miniature white wine and my shiny-new-totally-unfancy laptop (I've accidentally bought one that is absolutely massive. It's certainly not very portable and it's actually too big for my lap despite its name, oh and it's definitely NOT a Mac), so I'm good to make a start.

The 'Gang'

My earliest memory is when my sister Martha was being born. Nobody believes me, and you won't either, but I was 20 months old and sat in the back of a car with my dad's mum, Grandma Doris. (Yes, she's called Doris, ledge.) I remember being sat next to her, when my dad pulled over to have a massive row with a man who had a huge moustache. That's all I remember. Years later I told my mum that and she said that was when Martha was being born. I swear to God, to this day I remember that. I thought my dad was a hero because he shouted at the big hairy tash man who was scaring me and Grandma. (Although Doris would have absolutely obliterated him if push came to shove. She once grabbed two blokes by the scruff of their necks who broke into her home, whacked them with her gold walking stick and locked them in the bathroom. She's from Pontefract. Don't worry about it.)

My brother George soon came along, a year after that. I don't remember him being born, but story has it he was so massive that he had to be seriously sucked out by his head, which makes sense because his head is honestly the biggest head you will ever see on a human being.

So, there were three of us. Emily, Martha and George. We sound like a load of Victorian orphans. Martha is very organised, insanely smart, and utterly hilarious. She is extremely compelling, and strong-willed. Anybody who meets her never forgets her. She's powerful, yet really warm – I think it's quite special to have a solid balance of the two. People call it 'middle child syndrome' because the middle one is often left to fend for themselves slightly more than if they were born first or last, and I think that has always worked in Martha's favour. Since we were kids, she has always been getting me out of the shit. (She now happens to be my agent, so definitely still getting me out of the shit. But at least I can finally pay her to do it.)

In case I haven't made it clear enough yet, I bloody love her. She's my twin soul. You know the way twins say they can feel it if the other one has hurt themselves, or they get a strange feeling when one of them is in trouble or upset by something? We're convinced we can do that. Martha has called me some mornings knowing that I've had a rough night's sleep, or that something's troubling me: 'I'm getting a twin vibe … what's wrong?' It's bizarre!

Then there's George. He's a six-foot-one, very hairy, guitar-playing veggie who loves to travel and cook and garden. His phone is always smashed to pieces and he loses his bank card every weekend but he will give you the Black Sabbath t-shirt off his back and make you howl with laughter at any given opportunity. Everybody adores being in George's company because he has that skill of making you feel like you're the only person in the room when he's talking to you. He's like a hungover Jesus. It took him a while to find his feet in life, and he certainly had his struggles. Put it this way ... the police used to describe him as 'a joy to arrest'. George was always, ALWAYS in trouble. But his charm and kindness have always won people over in the end.

Being three siblings born within a few years of each other meant an unbreakable closeness; despite the variety of head sizes we were like triplets. We shared a bedroom (Martha and George in a bunk and me in the corner in a very over-the-top double bed like a diva). We played nicely together, we got bollocked together. A trio of different personalities united by our sense of humour – and god, we were loved. Our parents smothered us with love.

Mum and Dad. Wow, where to even begin. Let's start with Mum.

My mum, Kate, raised on the Wirral, now queen of jazz bars in Soho, was once described as 'one hell of a woman' by a fan who came over to her at one of her shows. I was about nine at the time, and I remember thinking that was a perfect way to describe her. Mum's first big break in showbusiness was writing the song 'Surprise, Surprise' for Cilla Black. Later, her hit 'More Than In Love' got to number two in the charts. She went on to become an actress, impressionist, comedian, the lot. She's even represented the UK in Eurovision (they came third, smashed it). Her talents know no bounds and she's the most beautiful woman in the whole wide world. Okay, I know I'm biased, but seriously – she's utterly, wonderfully bonkers. (The anagram of Kate Robbins is 'a bit bonkers'.)

Dad. Keith – 'Keefy boy' as my mates call him. Born and raised in Pontefract, Yorkshire. A musician, a guitarist – a bit of a legend. My dad has been called handsome his entire life. As a kid, everyone would say to me he looked like Brad Pitt. Dad was part of the pop scene in the eighties; with his twin brother Tim they had a band called Child, and their biggest hit got to number ten in the charts. Not as good as Mum's number two, but what you gonna do? I'm just joking. Same as mum, my dad is an extremely talented musician. The guitar being his first love, but don't knock his piano playing – unreal.

Great for house parties. He has played in bands all around the world, and was Bonnie Tyler's guitarist for 25 years. I'll never forget going to watch him in this amazing tribute band for the Eagles and falling in love with their songs. (The Illegal Eagles. What a name!)

And that's the number one squad. The OGs. We called ourselves the 'Gang'. The five of us.

But really, we're a clan. Or as many a newspaper column has called us 'a showbiz dynasty' (lols). My life is blessed and cluttered with aunts, uncles and cousins. We are and have always been the closest family you could imagine, and, while I'm well aware that this is blowing my own horn here, I can promise you that you haven't truly lived until you've been to one of our parties. The good news is there's plenty of them to choose from – a Sunday roast can soon turn into a singing Sunday service like at Kim & Kanye's house – without the mansion. Our Boxing Day parties were particularly legendary growing up: hundreds of people would pile into our house, around the piano. My uncle Simon was a professional dancer and I remember him twirling all my aunts around the living room, winking at me and calling me Claudia – he'd tease me that I looked like Claudia Schiffer. Every year he'd line us up and choreograph dance routines for each of us. Just total joy. You have to come fully prepared for the tidal wave of booze, though. I'd advise milkthistle, alka-seltzer and the Monday off work. Famously, my aunt Lynne once slipped down the stairs on the balls of her feet carrying a drink in each hand and didn't spill a drop of either. That's a real Scouser for you.

Nowadays we sit in my aunty Amy's kitchen most weekends and have a laugh over a massive bowl of pasta and gallons of wine. My cousins are like siblings to me, and are the funniest people on the planet. Our family WhatsApp group is popping off every single day. We go from chatting about weekend away trips, to who we think would have the worst breath out of the *X Factor* judges.

And, okay, fair enough since you've asked, yes I *am* related to Paul McCartney. I'm sure he goes around bragging to all his friends about me (cough, cough). He's my grandma Betty's first cousin, second cousin to my mum. I have extremely fond, loving memories of Paul and his presence within the family growing up. He was very close to my grandma as she was there for him a lot when his mum, Mary, died. My grandma was a bit older and so really took him under her wing. She taught

12

him how to play the ukulele. It was her and my grandad Mike Robbins who suggested Paul and his friend John (Lennon) play in their pub, the Fox and Hounds during a busy lunch time. They called themselves the Nerk Twins. And it all pretty much took off from there! They would rehearse in my grandparents' garage, and play with my mum, her brother and three sisters and sort of babysit them while my grandparents worked in their pub downstairs.

We spent weekends at Paul's house in Sussex when we were young. I remember acres and acres and ACRES of land with horses. Linda took us out riding when she was alive; I only have very vague memories of Linda as I was so young, but I remember her passing away, I actually seem to recall it was probably the first death in the family I was aware of.

Paul is so warm and chilled and loving. He once had Martha on his knee singing 'Martha My Dear' to her, a song that Mum and Dad used to always sing to her too. She turned and said to him, 'Oh, you know that song too!' To which he replied, 'Know it? I wrote it!'

I remember how lovely his kids were to us as well. I have particular memories of Stella, Mary and

James. Apparently, I used to watch James shaving in the bathroom like a little weirdo. He told me a few years ago at a party that I used to do that. How embarrassing.

My grandma Betty, my mum's mum, was one of the most beautiful women ever to grace this earth. She and my grandad Mike met at Butlins in the early 1950s, when my grandad was working as a Redcoat. He instantly fell in love with Grandma. He made her enter beauty competitions and she won every time. 'Miss Holiday' was her last title, I believe! I'd love to say I was also awarded a similar title in Ibiza but it's a book and they'll fact check it, so I can't lie.

Grandma was the funniest woman I've ever known. Her toilet humour ensured she would howl with laughter every time someone mentioned anything to do with farting. Together we'd gawp at gorgeous Spanish men on holiday and giggle in the corner, while she sipped gin and tonics and reapplied her lipstick. You would never see Grandma without her face on, ever. It was part of her routine every single morning. I often think of her doing her mascara, holding her mirror in one hand and the wand in the other, with a pouting concentration face as she applied it. Her skin was so soft and she always smelt of lavender. I can still smell her. Always laughing, always joyous, and just the kindest, most softly spoken and non-judgemental woman ever. She was a Samaritan for a long time, so she was perfect to talk to about any problem you had. I, of course, always spoke to her about boys.

She sadly got very poorly and deteriorated quite quickly in 2007. We sat around her bed in my aunty Amy's house and said our goodbyes, all of us together, as she passed. I remember clutching onto her body when she'd gone. I couldn't bear the thought that it was the last time I was going to see her and tell her how much I loved her.

My grandad Mike … what a man he was! The funniest man in the world. Utterly hilarious. An original Butlins Redcoat, he was a die-hard Wrexham supporter, and he adored Grandma. They called each other 'Percy' – no idea why. My grandad would be in the kitchen and he'd call to her in the next room, as she sat doing a crossword, 'Can I get you anything Percy?'

They both took great delight in watching all their grandkids grow up and were intrigued to see what happened for us, as they had such eventful times with their own kids.

Sadly, a year to the day that my grandma had passed away, grandad died. It was an unusual day, everything happened so quickly. I'm sure our mum knows what happened to him physically but it was never discussed at great lengths. I realise now that because our lives are so full of love, when somebody passes, we grieve and we take our time to do so but the crux of that person's death isn't ever discussed in detail (I suppose, why would you?). He fell out of bed, and as a result of the fall became very unwell over a period of a few hours. He had laid on his bedroom floor for a while, unable to get himself up, an ambulance was called (I don't know by who) and he was taken to hospital. I remember some family were in the area but my aunt and uncle who he lived with were away. Martha and I were around (we still lived near home then) and were called by Aunty Amy to go and see if he was okay. We got to the hospital expecting him to maybe have a broken wrist, but the doctors said he only had a few hours to live and that we should get all the family there. They were some of the hardest hours I've ever been through in my life – making those phone calls to everyone. To my mum, aunts and uncles, telling them their perfectly healthy dad was about to die, and that they all had to get there as soon as possible. Grandad was still conscious when Martha and I were there, and I'm so lucky, but feel so guilty, that I got to hear his last words. The football had been on that day and he said to me, 'Did Wrexham win?' They hadn't, but I told him they had.

Not long after that he slipped into a coma-like state and Martha and I just sat there, holding his hands and stroking them and saying our good-byes. Everyone else made it in time, rushing back from where they were just before his heart stopped beating at exactly midnight, apart from my aunty Amy. My heart broke for her as she rushed in pleading, begging not to have missed him. He'd been gone for just a couple of minutes. Watching her sobbing and saying sorry over and over to him was utterly devastating. A wonderfully kind nurse looked at her and said, 'Your mother was calling to him.' I truly believe she was. A year to the day, just, a few minutes past midnight.

Out of everything that's happened so far in my life, I truly believe that the thing I'm luckiest for is my family. I like to think I have a little piece of all of them in me, but I worry that saying that sounds big-headed because then I would be describing myself as the best person on earth. But I really hope I've picked up some of their kindness and generosity.

Together we've been through the most incred-ible times, but there's also been tragedy. We've lost people along the way, some sooner than expected, but our strength as a family knows no bounds. We'd go to the ends of the earth for each other, and always find a smile, glass of wine, and a party at the root of anything, whether it be for happy or sad reasons. Being together has always got us through anything.

My parents got divorced when I was 16. It was hell, but they're still very much together now. Not in terms of a romantic relationship or anything – my dad is happily settled with his girlfriend Claire, who my mum also loves. And they have a beautiful little girl, Nancy, our half-sister, who is the absolute best and very much involved in our lives. But they are together as friends, together as respectful humans who raised three children and gave us the lives we had, and now have. They are best friends. And they are a wonderful example of how it can be even after a messy and sad divorce. If you can let go of anger, bitterness, guilt and regret, and just cherish the good times; let go of grudges and look at the bigger picture. Was my mum and dad's marriage a successful one? Hell, yes it was. Divorce doesn't make it unsuccessful. Their marriage was just a part of my parents' 'journeys' that had come to an end. But everything else carries on; they will be our parents forever. That love will never die.

Growing Up

I guess you could say our childhood wasn't like other people's. My parents were off touring a lot of the time. Touring, working, filming. Sometimes we got to go with them which was really fun – before the days when parents were fined for taking their kids out of school, we'd often be found watching Dad from the side of the stage at a Bonnie Tyler gig. I remember thinking once, 'Wow ... I can't believe all these people are here to watch my dad!'

I remember Mum being away more – not because she actually was, I just remember the feeling of it. I missed her! She worked her arse off to put a huge gorgeous roof over our heads and I would never make her feel bad for that. But I did miss her a lot, and I clung onto the moments of being with her when she was around. I think when you're little those things seem more extreme and you are way more sensitive to them, so she probably felt she was around enough. When she was away, we were very lucky to have a wonderful nanny, or child minder as my mates called her: Paula. Paula was an angel to us all, and still is! She was wiping my arse then, and she still pretty much wipes my arse now. She's basically become Bedfordshire's most sought after child minder, because she's absolutely excellent at it.

I missed Mum in all sorts of ways, but one of the things I was always praying for was the total thrill that she might be there to pick me up at the school gates. I would come out of my classroom imagining in my head that she'd be there to surprise me. She worked in London so couldn't really. That didn't happen very often, but I remember one morning she told me she was going to pick me up at the end of school, and I spent the day telling all my little mates that she was coming. (We were all little because we were children, just to clarify. I didn't have a group of friends who were especially small.)

I was SO excited. The bell rang and we walked out of our classroom. In my head it was always a bit like when you come out of the arrivals door at the airport, and everyone's lined up waiting and you feel dead famous as you walk past. And this time when I walked out, there she was. Tight leather trousers, tight leather jacket, massive-heeled boots, ciggy on the go, full face of make-up, and jet-black gorgeous hair. Still looking like an eighties rock star. And boy did she stand out like a sore thumb next to all the other mums, who would all tut at her and drag their husbands as far away as possible. My heart leapt with pride. 'DARLING!!!!!' she said, arms outstretched, and I ran into her arms as fast as I could. She always smelt of Elizabeth Arden flawless finish foundation, CK One and chewing gum. That smell of my mum will forever be my oxygen.

But for the most part, it all felt normal: it was our ordinary. We'd be running around the living room as kids, showing off in front of whoever might have come round for dinner or those who were there recording some tracks in my dad's studio. I remember once being pretty much butt-naked apart from my little pants, trying on Bonnie's high heels. She was so lovely to us, and we'd spend lots of holidays at her villa in Portugal.

One night – a school night – Paula put us to bed but then Mum and Dad arrived home, having been away. Mum gently woke me up and told me to get dressed and put my favourite 'lady shoes' on because we were going out for dinner. (My lady shoes were this red pair I was only allowed to wear for special occasions. They had a tiny heel and made cloppy sounds – I LOVED wearing them.) They took all of us to an Indian restaurant just up the road. It was probably only nine o'clock but it felt magically like the middle of the night to me. I remember swinging my legs back and forth because my feet

23

didn't touch the ground, as Mum said I could have whatever I wanted. I'd tried Chinese spare ribs for the first time a few nights before but thought they were Indian, so kept trying to describe to the waiter what they were. He kindly kept bringing me out dishes and I kept sending them back. Now when I think about it, I can't believe Mum let me do that – but I think she was so desperate to give me what I wanted because occasions all together like that were so rare. I felt so lucky, and was probably the only kid at school to reek of garlic naan the next day, nodding off in maths.

We lived in a beautiful house. The Old School. It was called that because it genuinely used to be a Sunday school about a million years ago; it was also a church at some point. It was huge, dusty, bricky, covered in ivy and red and orange roses, with a big garden and an electric gate at the end of the pebbled driveway. Inside, it was a gorgeous mess. I hate myself for always moaning about the chaos, because when I think of it now, I'd give anything to go back there. Okay, sure, you couldn't find a pair of matching socks, and not a single sod knew how to work the TV. We had about a million remotes for each one, which we called 'the knobs'. (When I would ask, 'where's the knobs,' if I was at a friend's house for tea I'd be met with odd stares from my mate's mum.) And once you lost something, you knew you'd never see it again. The house was like a Bermuda Triangle, but dustier.

The thing that always makes me laugh looking back is that there were about eight bedrooms in that house, and yet me, Martha and George insisted on sharing one room together until I was about 13. We didn't want to separate. I had a queen-size bed, and Martha and George had bunk beds. Absolute chaos. Getting bollocked every 20 minutes because instead of sleeping, we were taking it in turns to jump off the top bunk onto my bed – we mastered the art of moving it to a perfect position to jump onto in order to get the best bounce. We would cry with laughter until really late and be little tired bastards in the morning when we had to get up for school. We missed the bus every single day and were always the last ones to turn up to registration. Everyone called us 'The Osbournes'. I kinda liked that!

The village we grew up in was a hamlet called Tebworth, in Bedfordshire. It was so tiny. It had one pub, a post office, and a really long lane that led to loads of crop fields and streams. We'd walk our dog, Rosie, down the lane with Dad at the weekends, and play 'cow splat': Dad would find the biggest cowpat and chuck a huge brick into it to see how far the shit would go. The idea being that us kids would all get covered in poo. It was hilarious. We'd get back home ruined and Mum would kick off. Great Saturday. Or Shaturday. Or SaTURDay. Sorry.

To everyone else, it must have seemed like we had a perfect life. And, in a sense, I guess that's true. I knew we were fortunate. Things were mad, but we were loved. I really want that message to be clear: we could not have been more loved. But as you get older, you become more knowledgeable, more aware of cracks, more aware of pain, and more aware that – actually – things weren't perfect like you thought they were.

From a very young age, I knew my dad was very much noticed by other women. Women at parties, at the shops, even friends of my mum's. I always noticed it and I hated it. I followed my dad around like an annoying little shit just double-checking nobody was trying to steal him from my mum. I guarded him and stared at women who I thought were trying to get my dad's attention. I think later on in life this little girl definitely practised the same behaviour with boyfriends. But we'll get to that later.

My parents loved each other. The one thing that was never lacking between them was laughter.

They would laugh and laugh and laugh, clutching their wine glasses in one hand, their stomachs in the other, while they wheezed and rocked. You know, that sort of laugh you get with your best mate in assembly when you think you might just pass out because you actually can't breathe. Sometimes I would sneak downstairs and sit just outside the main living room where they would be watching TV, laughing at *Parkinson*, or watching films, or I'd simply sit and listen to them chatting and laughing. Sometimes they'd catch me and let me sit with them for half an hour before I went up to bed. (That's how I first saw the film *Wayne's World* and it became one of my fave films of all time. Excellent!)

I would often sneak downstairs to try to persuade them to let me stay up with them for a bit. I wanted my own private 'eldest daughter' time with them while Martha and George were asleep in bed. I came downstairs once when Mum was away (knowing it was more likely that Dad would let me stay up), and he was making a quick dinner for himself as he'd got in late. He showed me step by step how to make it. It was a melon and Parma ham salad with a homemade dressing, loads of chopped things in it. I think this was when my love of food started! I loved all the colours of the vegetables and fruit, and bloody loved eating it. My dad is an incredible cook. He always made such a mess in the kitchen and it irritated the life out of Mum.

Our kitchen really was the heart of the home. It was huge and old and full of happiness when it was crammed full of people. It makes my heart physically hurt to think of it. From our fifth birthday parties, to the teenage booze-fuelled gatherings we had when our parents were away. The parties my parents had with family, neighbours, and every now and then a more work-based do where loads of celebs would come. I remember once our neighbour came storming into the house shouting, 'Whose bloody gold car is that on my drive?!' Then Des O'Connor poked his little head from around the corner of the kitchen and sheepishly put his hand up. Gutted, Des. (I swear that's completely true.)

All of this together probably gives you the impression that from the off I was quite precocious. I guess I could be both of those things in front of the people who knew me best, but I was actually really self-conscious growing up. Which was weird because ever since I can remember having thoughts, I knew that I was going to be in the entertainment world in some way. It was inevitable. I'd seen my mum be a famous actress and I guess, in some ways, I just really wanted to be like her. It was like repeat behaviour.

And, if I'm honest, I also wanted to be famous – for all the decent reasons, if there are any. I liked the idea of being admired and people knowing my name.

It was singing that got me first. I remember hearing Céline Dion when we were having tea at Paula's house one day. I was about six or seven and I thought to myself, 'Oh my God, how does that lady get her voice like that?' I gave it a go. The look on Paula's face was priceless, I still remember it now. She told me to do it again, so I did. I remember thinking, 'Oh, I can sound a little bit like that lady.' It was probably the first impersonation I ever did, but not my last! I love doing impressions; nailing a person's inflections and mannerisms is so much fun. I still do Céline on karaoke. But even then I didn't want to be anyone else. I didn't want to be Céline Dion or Whitney Houston or any of the other greats. I wanted to be Emily.

Saying that, I bloody loved me a persona. For a bit I was Tracey the pop star. I liked playing with my mum's lip gloss and, as soon as the wand brushed over my lips, it was like a spell had been cast. Over the speakers (in my head), a voiceover would play introducing me to the audience, and I'd whip my little blonde head round and look directly into the make-believe camera. My other go-to was Lola Red. Which, yes, I know, sounds a bit like a porn star name now.

But it was weird because I really was quite a shy child. All of this performing wasn't for anyone's benefit except mine and the bathroom mirror's. Mum would try to get me to sing for the neighbours when she and Dad threw their parties and I hated it. Singing felt too much like baring your soul, which is maybe why I settled more on acting in the end.

The first play I was in was *A Midsummer Night's Dream* when I was 12. I played Titania and it was a musical version: there was a big ballad and I won the drama award that year for it. That sticks out because I wasn't the best at school – for lots of reasons – and that was a dose of recognition that I was good at something. I wasn't *too* naughty or anything; I just wasn't fussed about sitting in a stuffy classroom, listening to things I didn't care about from teachers who I was pretty sure didn't care about them either. The subject I was always best at was boys – which is ironic, really, because they're still something I'm trying to figure out.

The People
Who Shaped Me:
The Cousins

As soon as I sat down to think about what was going to go in this book – a book about all the things that have got me to 29 years young – I realised that, if I was a ready meal, the packaging would read 'Emily Atack (60%)'. The remaining 40% is made up of weird and wonderful people and a glug of dry rosé wine. Those weird and wonderful people have looked after me, cared for me and gifted me some of their spirit. So, throughout the book I'm going to dot little spotlight pieces on some of these amazing people and how they've shaped me. And the first lot I want to shine a light on are my wonderful cousins.

Cousins are the best invention since the see-through Game Boy. They are basically 50 per cent sibling, 50 per cent mate. You look the same but different. You understand each other on a deep, deep level, and you have a smidgen more social etiquette towards them than your brother or sister. It makes me really sad for my friends who don't have that relationship with their cousins, because mine were the first best friends I ever had. They are still my best friends to this day.

The fact that your parents are also siblings is

often forgotten, but it's actually pretty cool when you stop and think about it. I think about me, Martha and George and when (one day, God willing) we have kids, I imagine our children being friends and my heart swells. Having so many aunties and uncles means I have a long line of first cousins who range from 13 to 36 and, to put it simply, there are no people on this earth I'd rather spend my time with. They are an eclectic mix of everything I love about people.

Most of them have northern accents like our parents, are model-tall, and they are all absolutely gorgeous. Growing up, we would spend spring days terrorising each other in a spare bedroom of my grandparents' house in Birkenhead, locking the smaller ones in bathrooms, nearly decapitating each other hanging out of windows and throwing sweets in the road. We slept in dens on the floor of each other's bedrooms, we stayed up late and ate midnight feasts until we were sick. We were bollocked on car journeys for swearing at bus drivers. We went to theme parks, sweet factories, Santa's grottos, and have gone on holiday together. My cousin Lydia is my make-up artist and is with me every single day. She lives three minutes' walk away from my house. Lydia and her brother Henry lost their dad

Simon a few years ago – my gorgeous uncle Simon. Simon was a choreographer, and danced for the greats like Diana Ross and Cliff Richard. Later in life, he was *the* Tinky Winky from Tellytubbies. Yep. You couldn't make it up. He was the guy inside the suit. Unreal! He was, is, such a huge compelling spirit in our family. Simon married my aunty Emma and gave us the gift of Lydia and Henry. He was gorgeous, inside and out. Watching the unimaginable grief they experienced was unbearable; all us cousins would stay up late messaging each other, asking who had checked in that day, asking who was seeing them that weekend.

They've taught me openness, love, friendship – things that I've looked to create with all my other friendship groups. They're my solid foundations that everything else is built upon and it doesn't matter what happens in the rest of my life – if all the walls are knocked down, I know those foundations will still be there. They make me think of those Ellie Goulding lyrics: 'When I'm standing with you, I'm standing with an army.'

The cousins have just started to have babies and there are weddings on the horizon. When Christmas comes around you'll find us girl cousins crammed onto a sofa, screaming, drinking fizz, talking about boys, laughing until we almost die. Even now, approaching 30, the thought of pulling into the driveway of an aunt's house for a birthday party, knowing the cousin crew are in; inside or in the garden – and thinking of that cheer of 'Wheeeey' as one more arrives – makes me laugh out loud.

They are the little added extra in my life, the bonus gold star in my sky. I couldn't live without them.

The Nineties
Best Bits

The TV was amazing – *The Queen's Nose, Goosebumps, Saved by the Bell, Sister, Sister, Sabrina the Teenage Witch.* I got a bit hot under the collar over *Neighbours* for a bit when I was very little. When we were a bit older, we'd stay up late on a Friday with next door's kids and Sky TV came along, WWE Wrestling (then WWF), The Box music channel and *Jackass* . . . then you'd flick over to Babestation for your first porn experience and scream at the girls twerking and chatting on their phones.

Tammy Girl – remember how amazingly slutty all the clothes were? Including the silky pyjamas. The photobooth in Tammy was well ahead of its time.

Sugar magazine – the Q and A pages were the best, and you could learn song lyrics from a back page of the magazine.

The internet – I mean pre-Insta, pre-iphone, house-phone internet. It took forever to load, cost hundreds of pounds to use, and there was that dial-up tone that sounded like you were going to the moon when you connected to it. No one could use it and make a phone call at the same time. It felt like an alien world.

Scented gel pens – caused no end of problems in middle school. Full gang wars over who had what scent.

Happiness was simply pens that smelt like grapes. Don't even get me started on the popcorn one . . .

Renting videos – we didn't have a Blockbuster near us, but the little convenience shop in the next village had a video rental bit at the back. Thrilling if we were allowed to rent one. It was a *bit * seedy, you'd go behind a curtain to find 3 walls of videos. Rude ones on the top shelf with ladies with their tits out on the cover. We almost always forgot to return them and had to pay a fine.

Beanie Babies – they were such a waste of money and yet we had millions of them. Again, another reason for many arguments and fall outs.

The Top 40 – it was on the radio on a Sunday and if you remembered to listen to it you could tape the songs you liked using a cassette.

Tamigotchis – except, okay, I never actually forgot about those very cute, utterly bizarre little digital pets. They were so great for the five minutes before you got bored with them.

The jelly aliens that live in goo – everyone would say that their one had given birth if you hold them together by their bums. It's a load of bollocks.

School Discos, youth clubs (always terrifying), Boys To Men ballads, Ben from A1's curtains, *Titanic*, playing Snake on the 3310... *sigh*

First Time
For Everything

First Kiss

I was ten, it was with a boy called James who lived next door to us. All the local kids would play down the crop fields – they were really fun days. We were all playing kiss chase one day and James kept going for me. I was chuffed cos I'd fancied him for about a week and liked playing with him, he was a good laugh. Sweet little ginger lad, looked a bit like Tintin. While we were playing kiss chase, he said to me, 'Have you ever got off with anyone before?' ('Got off' means 'snog', for anyone unfamiliar.) I said, 'Err, yeah, course, loads of times', and we agreed to count to three and give it a go. One … two … three. Then his little tongue hit my mouth and I was so mortified that I ran home, bright red, to have my tea. And I'll never forget my mum ACTUALLY said to me, 'You're all flushed, have you been kissing a boy?!' PAH, yeah right, Mum, chill out!! (Christ, she knew

me so well even then.) So not really a first KISS as
such. More of an embarrassing attempt that didn't go
to plan, which I don't blame James for. I bottled it.

First Actual Snog

I was about 11 and in a park that was near to my
house with some slightly older boys. I used to lie
about my age a lot so I could hang around with
the older kids. The boys were drinking cider and
running around pretending to be drunk. There was
one particular boy called Chris who I liked and he
was paying me some attention, and he then kissed
me out of nowhere. I've no idea how I blagged it,
but we were snogging for about an hour until my
little shite of a brother ran over and saw us and
thought it was the funniest thing he'd ever seen. He
said if Chris didn't buy him an ice cream from the
ice-cream van, he was definitely going to tell Mum.
I was on a bit of a roll and realised I was good at
snogging, so then snogged Chris's mate Kyle about
an hour later. So many ice creams bought for my
brother that day. And he still told Mum anyway and
I was banned from wearing make-up for a month.
Little prick.

First Fag

It was also when I was 11 that I started hanging around with an older girl called Stacey. Stacey was my idol growing up, my real-life Beyoncé. She was naturally pretty, tall, slim, had pale freckly skin and was always changing her hair colour. Essentially a mega-gorgeous chameleon. She introduced me to most things in life, a Benson & Hedges super king being one of them. Her parents were smokers and were out one day while we were at her house, so we nicked one of her mum's fags and had it out the back door to the garden. I watched her and copied how she did it. I held the smoke in my mouth and blew it out. It tasted rank but I liked the thrill of it so did this a few times with her and the older boys, until one day I accidentally took it down and inhaled the smoke … i.e. I accidentally smoked it properly – and promptly coughed my guts up.

First Drink

This is going to make me sound like I'm showing off. But the first time I ever got properly drunk was at a Paul McCartney concert. Because of the family connection we were in the VIP section, where there's always endless amounts of free champagne. I was about 12, but I looked 19, and I just kept secretly swigging the champagne. Because all my mum's side of the family are Scousers, the party vibes were in full flow and it was very easy to get away with being sneaky with the booze. I remember thinking, 'Oh wow, I think I'm actually drunk' … so then carried on and on. Next thing I knew, loads of aunties and Mum were gathered around me trying to pick me up, saying to each other, 'How much has she had to drink?!' Which I found hilarious because I was fine. I was having a great time! Of course, then I was sick ALL day the next day: my first hangover. It was also the first time I ever said, 'I'm never drinking ever again.' PAH! Kids, eh?!

The 'First Time'

Way too young. Painful, awkward, uncomfortable. Next.

First Thong

Stacey took me to a shitty little shopping centre when I was 11 or 12, where we'd hang around smoking with boys. She told me we were both going to go to New Look to buy a thong. I'd never worn one before. My mum had always said, 'Never wear thongs when you're older. You spend 15 quid on it and a tenner of it goes up the crack of your arse.' So I'd never seen the fascination with them. But Stacey stressed to me that it was the way to go, so I went into New Look with my £15 Mum had given me for the day (Mum thinking that I had gone to a car-boot sale with Stacey and her mum – still feel bad about that) and spent every penny on this tiny little black thong. I stood in the New Look queue absolutely certain that women were rolling their eyes and tutting at me. I felt like I was doing something illegal! And was also deep down completely gutted that I couldn't get a McDonald's on the way home because I was spending all my money on some stretchy black bum floss.

We both put them on when we got back to Stacey's and I had to pretend it wasn't hideously uncomfortable. Mum was SO right. Also, not worth the hassle of hiding it from your family. I managed to wash it myself so that nobody ever saw it and hid it in a special drawer, until one day my little brother got hold of it, was so horrified that he chucked it out my bedroom window and covered it in washing-up liquid and shampoo. I was secretly pleased, it probably needed another hand wash. He then told Mum who was livid. News of my infamous thong managed to reach the school and so the rumours began. Boys would sometimes ask about it. If they were lucky I used to give them a nudge and show them the strap - I should probably have bought more than one.

'Tom'

Then there's my first love. This deserves a whole chapter and … well, it's not the happiest of stories, for lots of reasons.

I was 13 and had just started Upper School. Things weren't exactly going great. My parents' marriage was on the rocks by this point, and I was being bullied at school by a group of really scary girls in the year above.

I'd been at the school for a couple of weeks before I started to notice a lad called Tom. Tom was two years above me. About five-foot-six, dark curly hair, blue eyes, skateboard glued to his left arm, and so many wristbands that covered every rock band you can think of. Tom stood out from everyone else. He was loud, hilarious, usually had something obscene written on the back of his school blazer, and was ALWAYS getting bollocked by a teacher in the corridor.

I was instantly drawn to Tom. I looked at him and genuinely thought, 'I want him to be my boyfriend.' I'd had crushes on boys since I was in nappies, but I'd never had this feeling before. Every time I saw him, or he walked past me or I heard his laugh,

I felt like I was on that ride at Alton Towers. The Oblivion, where you literally get dropped from a terrifying height into the ground and every single organ in your body feels like it's going to come out of your arse. (Horrific – yet thrilling – and you obviously go on it again.)

By about a month into being at the school, I'd pretty much worked out Tom's routine of where he hung around, what sort of times he'd be walking back from the tennis courts with the smokers, what time he would be in the lunch hall, and who his closest allies were, etc. (Not that I was his stalker or anything. I was just your average teenage, psychopathic girl.)

I was on my way to registration after lunch, doing my usual slightly longer route. This took me past his form group, who had to stand outside their classroom in a line before going in, so I always got a glimpse of him. When, suddenly, there he was blocking my path and held out his hand to shake mine. 'Hi, I'm Tom.' Oh God. Oh sweet Jesus. Holy mother of Moses. I was on the Oblivion again, that slow-motion bit of being carted horizontally up to the top of the ride, where you sort of feel like you're slowly being led to your death, but you are far too intrigued not to take the plunge.

I froze. I think I mustered a 'Hi', probably an embarrassing croaky one, and then I walked on. I went home and logged into MSN (Em_Is_Bad@mail.com, if you're asking) and asked around if anyone had his MSN address. I found it, and added him. Now, for legal reasons, I obviously can't share his email address with you. Not because I'm scared of getting in trouble but because it was almost as shocking as Em_Is_Bad@mail.com But I typed it out just so I could look at it, and I mean this with every inch of my soul that when I see it written out, to this day, I STILL feel like my bowels are going to collapse.

I remember the first time he signed in. I thought I was going to be sick. It sounds so ridiculous but this is honestly how he made me feel, all the time. I didn't speak to him, didn't dare. So I was thinking of ways to ensure that another exchange would happen where I wouldn't be a quivering mess, and I would actually start a conversation so we could begin falling in love.

I found out about a night that was happening in Bedford, a 'battle of the bands'-type night. There were flyers going around school, and Tom came over to me and handed me one and asked me to come, his band were playing. I managed to muster some kind of over-the-top nonchalant response, and went home that night and begged my mum to let me go. I did the whole 'Mum, everyone is going apart from me, the school have put it on so it's not like we can drink or anything!' routine, which was kind of true (you just had to be 16 to go, and I'd just turned 14). But I'd promised Mum and Dad I'd stay with my friends, and would only drink a maximum two blue WKDs, and they could pick me up at a respectable 10pm.

It was a Friday night, and I'd spent hours and hours getting ready. I was so excited I couldn't even eat my tea. My mum knew there was a boy involved, and so she bought me a new top to wear and new shoes. The bullying at school had become quite bad, and so she was essentially treating me to this night out as I'd been having a tough time. She gave me £20 and dropped me and my (very reluctant) friends off in Bedford. We arrived at the place. Utter shitehole, but I didn't care. Hardcore rock music blaring from the stage, blokes and women with huge red mohicans, tattoos and piercings. The smell of fags, beer and actual poo lingering on the graffiti-stained walls, while young lads moshed onstage, screaming into microphones about blood and hating their dads. I think some of the dads were even stood there watching, with their pints in massive plastic cups.

I stood out like a sore thumb with my brand-new blue silk halterneck top, flared jeans and pale-blue pointy-heeled boots, with my long blonde hair and face plastered in make-up. People I recognised from the years above me at school whispering to each other, 'What the hell is Emily Atack doing here?' This was undoubtedly the place where the 'greebos' and 'goths' came. And I wasn't in that category at school. So I had a lot of Marilyn Manson lookalikes glaring at me and shouting, 'All right, Barbie!' Time to neck a WKD.

WKD necked, and a few moans from my friends later, Tom came onstage and introduced his band. I stood at a pretty bloody good 'playing it cool' spot so that he could see me but not too obviously. My stomach was churning, and I started to think about my tea that I hadn't eaten earlier. I had another WKD, of course taking a sip every time I felt Tom's eyes on me. The band finished. I have no memory of them being good or not, I was just working out a tactic in my head the whole time for how I was going to see or speak to Tom afterwards without looking too desperate.

My friends were begging to leave but I begged them to stay just so that I could say hi to Tom.

To my amazement, he came straight over to me; we chatted a bit and he asked if I would like to go somewhere with him outside so we had a bit more privacy. I nearly ruptured a kidney with excitement, told my friends I'd be five minutes, and we walked outside. We found a kind of romantic dark doorway round the back of the bar that smelt mostly like piss. He opened a beer with his teeth and offered me one. I sort of pretended to sip one while he lit a fag, and we chatted. I can't really remember what we chatted about, but I remember thinking I was the luckiest girl in the whole world. I was talking when, out of nowhere, he kissed me. My heels made me taller than him, so I remember leaning into the wall and slouching down a bit so that we were the same height. This wasn't my first kiss (high-five, Chris), so I knew what I was doing. I felt like our mouths matched perfectly. He tasted of beer and fags, and I fell in love with him there and then. We kissed for a long time, and his hands were sort of touching my bum and up my back. My heart was pounding. I couldn't believe it was happening. And I was already terrified about losing him.

I had loads of missed calls from my friends and it was nearly 10pm, so I had to go. He walked me back to the bar holding my hand. Everyone was whispering and staring. I was chuffed to fucking bits. My friends were chuffed for me too, so I was forgiven for disappearing for an hour.

Tom said he'd text me when he got home, but then realised he didn't have any credit. I gave him a tenner from the £20 my mum gave me so that he could buy credit, and then he wouldn't have an excuse not to text me.

So the texting and MSN-ing began that weekend and, by Monday, every single person at school had got wind that we'd had a snog. It was front-page news of the imaginary school tabloids, everyone was talking about it. Even the teachers! (Made that bit up. They probably were, though.) The downside was it pissed off a lot of girls who fancied him, which didn't help the bullying situation.

He wasn't making a massive fuss of me at school just yet. He came over to say hi every now and then, but it was still quite tame. Then one night, he invited me to another one of his gigs and asked if he could stay over at mine afterwards as I lived closer to the venue. It took some persuading, but my parents eventually said he could stay – as long as he slept downstairs in the living room. Fair enough.

I went to the gig with a friend. It was basically just a massive piss-up in a hall full of hammered teenagers. Tom came straight over to me and snogged my face off in front of everyone. I was absolutely thrilled. (I should flag that by this point I had upped my greebo game slightly, so I didn't look too out of place. This basically involved me dressing more like Avril Lavigne rather than Britney Spears.)

I watched Tom's band play and, at the end of the gig, I noticed a dark-haired girl hovering around him. Flicking her hair, offering him fags. He was paying too much attention to her for my liking! So I asked him what time he wanted to go back to my house, seeing as he was staying. He turned to me and said he didn't need to stay over anymore, and he was going to go to another party with some friends. I felt like I'd been punched in the stomach. I knew he was staying because of this girl, and it made me want to die there and then. I got a taxi home and sobbed and sobbed. I knew at this point this wasn't going to be an easy ride. So I ended it and found a nice boy to go out with instead who was worth my time. Except obviously I did not do that.

After a few of these gig nights in a load of shit-holes, Tom and I became a proper boyfriend and girlfriend. On days where he wanted to pay attention to me, I was the happiest girl in the entire world. On the days where he ignored me, I went into myself and thought my world was ending.

He started to stay over at my house a lot. We weren't allowed to sleep in the same bed but I would sneak downstairs when my parents were asleep and be with him. I then started to stay at his and had to sleep in the spare room, but this time he'd do the sneaking and we'd stay in bed together for as long as possible. I felt completely addicted to this boy and needed him, and needed to be close to him.

One night, Tom's parents were out and we went up the road to his friend's house. The friend was older and had his own flat, where Tom and all his mates would hang around. Boozing, smoking weed, watching porn. Tom gave me some WKDs. Considerably more than I would usually drink. I was downing them and the lads were cheering, which obviously spurred me on to drink more.

I began to drink more and more. I would go to parties with Tom, we'd camp out in fields with all his friends, we'd sneak out of his house and go to all kinds of places where drinking and all sorts was involved. My parents tried to keep eyes on it all but I was just behaving how I wanted to by this point. I'd become so distant and withdrawn from my parents, who were by now having a really difficult time. I thought it best to just shut them out and stay with Tom as much as I could.

The bullying was making my school life extremely difficult. They'd spread awful rumours around about me, stick pictures of me up around all the villages with my mobile number on it – so I was getting abusive phone calls constantly. They were pushing me in the corridors, spitting at me, threatening me. I always told Tom about this but he pretty much ignored it and didn't do much to show sympathy or to help me. He'd left school by this point, so there was a degree of separation from the situation; maybe he didn't know how bad it was. Maybe he did and didn't think it was his problem.

I heard all kinds of rumours that he was cheating on me. That he'd shagged someone in a car park, shagged someone at a party, shagged his hair-dresser regularly. Girl after girl after girl. People would tell me on MSN, or at school. Some girls even claimed to my face that they were the person he'd been with.

Every time I'd hear something new, a part of me completely died. I'd scream at him, be physically sick, and then stay with him. This happened over and over. He even broke up with me on a few occasions accusing me of being a psycho, but I would do drastic things in order to make him get back with me. I drank a bottle of vodka and cut my wrists at a party once – a cry for help, a cry for attention, a cry for Tom's attention. Looking back, I was spiralling. I was too young to cope with my breaking heart and cloudy drunk head. I woke up with massive bandages on my wrists and had to hide them from my family. I was hiding more and more from them now. My mum would beg me to open up and speak to her but I just couldn't. She started to see cuts on my arms and it broke her heart. I'll never forgive myself for harming my body in that way, and to this day I still have no idea why I did that. I didn't want to die. I just felt so out of control of everything and it was almost like a 'fuck you everyone, cos I can do this if I want!' sort of thing. A rebellion, I guess. I was also so terrified of losing Tom I saw it like I had no other choice. So I guess that was why. Even just writing all of this, these awful feelings of emptiness come rushing back to me. The excited rush of the ride was over, and I was just left with emptiness and fear. I felt like I'd been left at the bottom of the Oblivion ride completely alone and it had broken down. I couldn't see how I would ever get out of this darkness again.

I was about 15 by this point. I'd lost a lot of weight, and I was constantly in trouble at school. Bunking school to avoid it because of the bullying, and hanging around with older people doing older things. My mood had changed and I was always snappy with my parents. I just felt so sad, SO sad and heartbroken ALL the time. I was having house parties the second my parents were away, hundreds of people in the house, every single room occupied with people, smoke, girls with their boobs out, people puking, the lot. The house was getting trashed every weekend and the neighbours were slowly starting to despise us. People still talk about the parties in that house to this day. I hope to God those walls never, EVER start talking.

You might read this and think it all sounds dramatic, and that every teenager feels the same, and actually getting your heart broken by a lad and your parents divorcing when you are this age is very common. Which is true, it does happen a lot. If it happened to you and you still feel shit about it, like I do, then I'm sorry. If it happened to you and you got over it straightaway, then hats off to you. When you're in the thick of the storm of teenage heartbreak, weathering a hormone hurricane, you don't think it will ever end. I think of the girl I was,

Britney Spears dressed as Avril Lavigne. Sipping a WKD. Desperate for Tom to love me, for the scary girls to leave me alone. There are a number of things that happened in that period that will stay with me forever. Some things I'm not ready to recall publicly yet.

By 16, my dad had moved out, things were at their worst, and it felt like I was shut inside the washing machine on a never-ending cycle of emotionally distressing madness. I would say 16 was my toughest age to date. I felt like my life had fallen apart at times, and I was trapped in it. And then I met Daniel.

'Daniel'

By 17, I'd managed to ditch my toxic relationship once and for all, and Martha and I were hanging around with a really hilarious and fun group of boys. I'd been at school with them but they were a couple of years older than me, and it was only after I left at 16 that I'd had the chance to get to know them properly. They really looked out for me and gave me some of my strength and confidence back. They also looked after me, my sister and brother through my parents' divorce, taking us all under their dusty, smoky, but really warm and friendly wings.

We would often go to my friend Jim's parents' house because it was massive and they were always away. We'd play beer pong, smoke, listen to music and piss ourselves laughing in the garage until the early hours of the morning most weekends. I felt safe around them. They'd take me to the pub and we'd play pool, darts, and they showed me how to use the fruit machines.

My parents had pretty much left Martha and me to our own devices at this point because they knew we were safe and staying out of trouble. It was right in the middle of the divorce. Dad was living elsewhere, and Mum was trying to sell the house. I was having drunk sex with a lot of morons outside of my friendship group, thinking that this would lead me to another boyfriend. It didn't.

Then, one day, the boys introduced me to a lad called Daniel. I'd known of Daniel a bit at school. He was loud, obnoxious, cocky, very bright, but a massive bellend in my opinion. He was perfect. We got on instantly and sat in the corner of the pub saying how we couldn't believe we'd never actually spoken before, at school. I fancied the absolute arse off him. He would drive me around in his grey Nova with one white door; we'd listen to Dizzee Rascal's first album, *Boy in da Corner*, on replay (one of the best albums ever – get it on immediately) and we started snogging in his car every night and getting takeaway pizzas at our friends' houses. We completely fell in love.

Underneath the madness, Daniel was kind, sensitive, intelligent, ambitious, and he treated me like I was the only woman on the earth. He utterly adored me, and I adored him. He made me see what real love was, and saved me from what I thought it was. He was pretty much living at our house in Tebworth and actually took on quite a strong parental role in the family as my dad wasn't around at that time. He was great with my brother and sister, cooked us lovely dinners, and, because he was training to be a carpenter, he was very useful around the house. He also later trained our dog, Snowie, who we inherited after the passing of my grandad Mike. She was a bichon frise puppy who shat and pissed EVERYWHERE. I would watch Daniel chasing her up the road in Tebworth every time she escaped and he would quite literally jump in front of lorries for her. He was also wonderful with my mum. She loved him. They'd have slightly heated debates about silly things and my mum would just end up saying, 'Ah shut up, yer silly twat.' I felt like he was quite literally rebuilding my life again – slowly putting the parts back together, hammering in all the loose nails, sanding down the surfaces of our fatigued and weary hearts. (Jesus, I love an analogy.)

Just before I turned 18, I decided to move out of the Old School. My dad was giving up a flat that he'd been living in about ten minutes from where we lived and said I could have it for a couple of months for free until I found substantial income that would mean I could start paying rent. Martha had only just turned 16 but I looked at her and said, 'Let's get outta here!'

My mum then decided to pack up our wonderful giant bastard of a house and moved out herself. Moving out of there was probably one of the most painful experiences of all our lives, and Daniel was there for me through every single last pointless, dusty hoarding item that I packed up, and he helped Martha and me move into our flat. Mum moved to London to have some space and recuperate and find more work, and our brother George moved in with my aunty Amy and my uncle Bob, as the flat we'd moved to was only a two-bed. Also, he was only 14!

So here were Martha and I, 16 and 17, living on our own. Completely legal, but absolutely fucking mental. We had all our mates over every night and things got a bit out of hand, but we were having the time of our lives. We'd be up till 2am most nights, all the boys taking it in turns to do the 24-hour McDonald's run in their Vauxhall Corsas. But I had Daniel, so I always felt some kind of security. Martha was working on the reception of a tanning salon to fund her own cheap wine and happy meals, while I was convinced that I was going to all of a sudden become a famous actress in a Channel 4 sitcom: that was my focus. And I wasn't letting anything get in the way of that. After banging some doors down, I soon bagged my part as Charlotte Hinchcliffe in *The Inbetweeners* (more on this shortly), which financially allowed Martha and me to fund our life-style. Then we got the news we'd all been dreading. My grandma Betty's cancer was spreading, and she didn't have long to live.

After a painful few months of standing by her bedside and holding her hand, we lost her. I will never forget how Daniel helped me/us through that. My poor mum felt her entire world had crumbled around her. I'll never forget her saying that losing her husband and her mum around the same time made her feel like she was free falling. I tried to imagine that level of grief, and it sums it up perfectly. I suspect it does feel that way. It was Daniel's strength, kindness and understanding that got me through it.

My beautiful grandma dying was kind of the final blow for us all in this particular period of time. It changed everything. Everyone went a bit mental for a couple of years. I was now 19, 20, and my career was in full swing when *Dancing on Ice* then came along. Sadly, it was the last straw for mine and Daniel's relationship. It wasn't just the time I spent away, but the life I was now living was simply a million miles away from him and the life we used to have. I disappeared up my own arse for that period of time. I was very young, earning tons of money, dancing with an American man every day, then touring the country after the whirlwind of the live shows.

I will always feel guilty about how I left Daniel behind in that time. He had done everything for me and everything he could to be with me, but my head was just completely somewhere else. I was terrified that if I didn't put everything I had into my career at this moment, I'd lose it all again. I was terrified of missing the boat. I had to grasp every opportunity with both hands if I wanted to survive in this business. So I was being selfish. So bloody selfish. And I'm sorry.

After a few painful and tearful chats and hugs, Daniel walked out of my flat. We were both sobbing. I knew we were doing the right thing, but I'll never forget the look on his face, and I'll never forget the emptiness I felt in my heart.

Daniel and I are still great friends to this day. He has a wonderful girlfriend and he's happy, and that makes me so happy too. We were two kids who were there for each other when we needed it. I will be forever grateful for people like him in my life.

The People
Who Shaped Me:
The Girls

Despite the temptation to write an entire chapter dedicated to the one and only *Friends* (the best sitcom of all time aside from *The Office*) I think I should instead dedicate some time to writing about the wonderful people in my life who I call my friends. Like sitcoms, friends come in all kinds of forms – some are broad, loud, brash and brazen. Some are crowd-pleasers. Some are cool, understated and dry but full of heart. Some friends last for 47 seasons, and some stick around for just two series and a Christmas special.

But when it comes to my girlfriends, I'm really lucky that I've had the same core group since I was miniature. There is my oldest school friend, Lou – married with two beautiful children now. She knew and loved my freckled face long before the jungle revealed it like it was new. She'd laugh at something about me that nobody else would notice. We know and love each other's families. We have together endured every colour of the friendship rainbow – from love to pain to grief. We have had hard times and travelled different paths, we are in fact entirely different people – but we have common ground and that's love.

are we there yet?

My best friend Skye was in my year at school
– Skye, Lou and I were a trio. Skye for me is that
friend who I would walk over hot coals for at four
in the morning even if she's a flight around the
world away – and vice versa. We all have one: that
girl who's been in your life since you were nine. The
one you sat next to in the school sandpit, and years
later sat next to in the GUM clinic on a hot Saturday
afternoon after a foolish night out in Nottingham,
or accompanied you to a Spanish police station to
obtain a crime reference number because you had
your iPhone 'stolen' on the first night of the holiday.
The girl who will walk behind you down the aisle
with tears in her eyes and fluff your veil. The girl
who, one day, will love your kids like her own – and
come round to take them to the park, because you're
on the lav with norovirus. Skye is that girl for me;
she doesn't half drive me up the wall sometimes but
she's part of my soul now. You know those cheap,
crappy fridge magnets that say, 'You'll always be
my friend – you know too much'? No one knows
this but I invented that saying for Skye.

Skye and I joined forces with my sister Martha's
friends in our teens (thank you mum for having
Martha and me so close together in age), and we've
not left their sides since. We call them 'the gaggle'

because it really suits them – they are like bumble-bees on a hot summer's day around a melting ice cream. They're all under five-foot-four and have been friends forever – Martha was very lucky to have them throughout her entire time at school. They are badly behaved, they live for bank holidays, ASOS orders and Ibiza trips; they love rooftop drinking in the summertime and Saturday nights watching *The X Factor* in the wintertime. They are the most supportive and loving girls I've ever met. They are obsessed with each other. They are nice to each other, they respect each other, they absolutely lay into each other. They might not always have the words, but they have the time, the time for me, they have the want for my company, they love my cooking, they love me and I love them. If my cousins are the foundations of my castle, the gaggle are my battlements on the roof – they lift me up and make me feel on top of the world. I love nothing more than treating the gaggle to a table in a nightclub with bottles of champagne and sparklers and watching them swarm excitedly around it.

Visually it's also a treat: Skye and I are taller than the gaggle, who call us old wenches (despite the fact that we're only about 12 months older than them). On a night out we are like the two big geese waddling to the pond with the line of goslings following clumsily behind and clucking at our knees.

It's my girlfriends who keep me centred and grounded. They make me whole.

My Big Break: Charlotte Hinchcliffe

Living on our own so young was surreal. I guess it was a bit like what you experience if you go to university at 18 – that first taste of freedom and the opportunity to not get dressed before 4pm (or at all), never do any washing-up or even think about cleaning the loo. Jokes! Aside from the debris of the parties we were quite well house-trained. Unlike uni, there wasn't a maintenance loan in sight and so, as soon as Martha and I moved in, I thought, 'Okay, I've got to start making shit happen now so I can look after the both of us.'

I had a job as a waitress and then in a call centre, and I was shocking at both, probably because I knew that what I really wanted to do was to act. Luckily, my mum's agent said he would take a chance on me. I remember him, dressed in one of his impeccable suits, weighing me up with his eyes and saying he'd send me out on some castings – there was no way I'd get any roles first time round, but if the feedback was positive then he'd take me on permanently.

And so, aged 17, I tottled off to my first ever audition, for the guest lead in an ITV crime drama called *Blue Murder*. In a way, Mum's agent telling me I was never going to get it made me way more confident. I'd learnt the lines till they were coming out of every orifice of my body, strode with my head held high into the room, and was told about a week later that I'd got the job. I couldn't believe it, but also I could: I'd come through so much by this point that I was ballsy as fuck, and ever since I could talk I'd always wanted to be a performer. It felt kind of like my destiny.

The part was a really young WAG-type girl called Kelly Lang. My first ever character. She was so much fun to play. My first day on set I remember being nervous – but Caroline Quentin, the star of *Blue Murder*, was lovely to me and she really took me under her wing. She taught me some of the technical aspects of it: shots and eye lines and all that sort of stuff.

Shortly after that, an audition came through for something called *Baggy Trousers*, a new comedy on E4. I read the script and I thought, 'Oh my God, this is really, really funny.' I was so hungry for it: one, because it was amazing; and two, because there is nothing that makes you hungry like the actual thought that you might soon run out of money and be hungry. Martha was working too, but we were scraping by and I desperately wanted to provide properly for us. The audition was for the main guy's wannabe love interest, a certain Charlotte Hinchcliffe, and it was in Twickenham. My mum said she'd drive me but then her car broke down. I remember the feeling of my stomach dropping away in disappointment, but then reasoning with myself that this was the second ever job I was going for, and it sounded too good to be true anyway – the likelihood that I'd get it was tiny. I was about to tell Mum that we should just leave it, when a really kind neighbour offered her car up so we could get there.

So by some magic we got to Twickenham and I met Nadira Seecoomar, the casting director. It was a really hot day so I was wearing a little white dress and had made myself up in the only way I knew how: full face of foundation and thick black eyelashes – I looked cracking, if I do say so myself. I did the audition and Nadira told me how great she thought it was. The feeling of that praise when I was only 17 and desperate to make it was incredible, I was so chuffed. But then she said to me, 'You're wearing far too much make-up.' So I thought, 'Okay, brilliant, definitely didn't get that then.'

But then I *did* get through to the next round. The audition was with the producers and the two writers: Iain Morris and Damon Beesley. This time I went prepared – no make-up whatsoever. As I went in, Nadira gave me a wink and said, 'That's better.' The audition itself was quite a naughty scene between a boy and a girl talking about sex, except the boy part was being read by a middle-aged woman. I remember thinking, 'This is very weird that I'm re-enacting this with someone who could be my mum.' I'm so used to doing that now, but it was quite funny that first time.

The third round was similar but with more people in the room – the closer you get to the prize, the more people from the production team come to watch. I remember saying in that third audition something I would never in a million years say now. But I wanted this part so much, I thought, 'This part could really change my life. I've got to pay rent, I *need* this job.' In a way I was just fearless – plus I didn't know any different. So I announced to the writers and everyone in the room, 'Nobody can do this part better than me. This part was made for me. Charlotte Hinchcliffe is made for me.'

They sort of nodded politely and laughed a bit and said, 'That's great. We're really glad you enjoyed the script.' Christ I was excited. I got a call later that day offering me the part.

Walking into the first read-through was an out-of-body-type experience. I felt like I had a belly full of bees; buzzing with excitement and nerves at the same time, sort of like a first day at school. And it really did feel like that because we were basically in a classroom – read-throughs are always in stuffy, cold village hall type places, otherwise known as 'rehearsal rooms' but it's basically a youth club. I pretended to make notes on my script because I saw other actors doing it. I remember I brought a pad and a pen, and I always wanted more than just the fruit and biscuits on the table (still do).

I was intrigued to find out who was going to be playing Will, because I knew he was the character I was going to be rolling around with in the bedroom and snogging. Then Simon Bird walked in and he fit the character description perfectly: cute, black curly hair and glasses. 'Okay, we can work with this,' I thought to myself. Ha! There was a big age difference of about seven years between us and I think he was slightly mortified about it, but I was quite mature for my age so it didn't bother me in the slightest.

We went round the circle and introduced ourselves and the characters we were playing – simple things like remembering how to speak seemed to kick in when it got to my intro – and then ...we made a start. I loved that first read-through. It was the first time I got to see the whole thing starting to come to life and even now I remember watching the chemistry between the boys and thinking they were great. It was at the read-through that I also met Emily Head, who played Carli – what a babe. We stuck together through the whole thing – she was so warm and friendly – and throughout the process all of us became good pals.

I loved going to work each day. I think sometimes, when you're watching TV, people don't stop to think of just how many people work behind the scenes on shows, but there are bloody loads of them, and the people who worked on *The Inbetweeners* were so nice. My make-up artist in particular made it such a nice experience. She was called Sarah Jane Hills and she was quite mumsy, and she made me feel at ease. I'd assumed they weren't going to let me wear make-up but had kept my fingers crossed that they might because of the character I was playing. And they did! I was the only actress who was allowed to.

One of the first scenes we had to do was the sex scene between me and Simon Bird. We were on location in a typically suburban house in Ruislip, west London, in a real teenage girl's bedroom. (What a claim to fame, eh? If it was *your* bedroom we shot in then I hope you put those sheets on eBay.)

My Big Break: Charlotte Hinchcliffe

Because it was the first time I'd ever done anything like it with a boy onscreen, I thought it was going to be really nerve-racking. But actually, in the end, I wasn't nervous at all and it was absolutely fine. *Obviously* – because who wouldn't want the opportunity to have a lovely gentleman like Simon Bird lie on top of them?! But seriously, I've found over the years that it's the guy who gets more nervous because there's obviously a certain thing that might happen which they can't control. Whereas I'm happy as Larry so long as I've got the flesh-coloured cups stuck to my boobs and sexy (it's not sexy) thong on. For most of the time when you're filming for something, you're standing around, freezing, in the arse end of nowhere, so getting to snuggle under a warm duvet chatting away to a nice boy has always been a part of the experience I've liked most!

I remember Simon climbing on top of me and he looked a bit nervy so I thought to myself, 'Right, I'm going to have to break the ice a bit here.' I went for: 'How does it feel being on top of a 17-year-old?'

He rolled his eyes at me. 'Oh, for fuck's sake. Thanks, Emily.' Lol.

We were a rabble. Most of the cast were pretty young and filming isn't an in-and-out job – the days are very long. If you ever remember going away on a school trip, it's that kind of vibe: you're around each other every second of the day, everyone's flirting and joking around. Joe Thomas, who played Simon, and Emily started going out which was really sweet. I struck up a particularly close friendship with James Buckley, who played Jay. We giggled all the time, he could really make me laugh. When you're young and you're working, it's nice to have someone you can cling onto a little bit – and James was that person for me. It never went any further than a couple of snogs at some wrap parties, but he was a good person to have around.

After the third series finished, we all went our separate ways. It's funny – when you're on a big job together, filming every day, you're in each other's pockets and you can't imagine not staying close friends with everyone. But when a series ends and everyone starts new projects, it's impossible to stay in touch like you did before. It was a bit of a shock then, but that's because it was my first big job. It's something I'm used to now. But maybe it was also a shock because that series was so important to me; it was such a massive part of my life for three years. It was my first major-part, and was where I learnt the ropes of the industry.

God, I'm grateful for kind neighbours and their cars.

Fame
(Not the Musical)

I'm quite grateful, to be honest, that my career kicked off before social media really got going. When I started out on *The Inbetweeners* people only cared about Facebook and Myspace – everything else was still pubescent, if you will. I'm not just grateful because I'm shit at it, but because I would have had no clue how to handle it. Going on TV doesn't come with a manual of how to approach that sort of stuff. Which is why when the first series aired and all these people began adding me as a friend on Facebook I went right ahead and accepted them. ALL of them. It was literally thousands – but I just thought to myself, 'Aw, this is nice, isn't it? Everyone wants to be my fwend.'

Then people started recognising me. Heads started turning a little bit; people would whisper when I was walking around shopping centres. They were more vocal about it on nights out or in pubs – then they'd come over and ask for photos. I quite liked it. I'd watched it happen to my mum all my life and so it was everything I'd wanted as a little girl. The only surprise was how quickly it could turn negative. For every ten people who came over, eight of them would be lovely but there'd be two who would be really nasty and say something awful. Weirdly, it was never girls – who I guess we always assume are quicker to be bitchy – it was men and boys.

But I could handle that. I can't really remember life before people being lovely and horrible to me at the same time. At school I had people either being nice to me or being absolutely vile. Whereas previously people had written things about me on the toilet walls, now they were in the newspapers. Fame seemed like an extended version of what I'd been through for years, except now I could afford loo roll.

That doesn't mean to say I was cool with everything that started going in the papers. It was eye-opening how much could be spun into a story. Not long after *Dancing on Ice*, I was stepping onto a road and a taxi pulled out and almost ran over my foot, so I knocked on the window to let the driver know I was there. A photographer snapped the whole thing and from the angle he was standing at, it looked like I was aggressively trying to smash the window in. The paper ran the headline 'ATACK ATTACKS A TAXI' – I was so shocked. If you don't do so already, take everything you read with a pinch of salt. But I did also think fair play to them because, come on, that's a pretty great headline.

The commentary on my body and my looks was worse. It was a really strange experience – because I suppose if a person slags you off, you actually never hear about it, do you? The point is, it's behind your back. Whereas when you're a celebrity, all the slagging off is in front of you. No one had ever called me fat before – a tart, a slut, I'd heard all of that sort of stuff, but I'd never thought there was anything wrong with my weight. Hearing the word 'fat' was painful, like someone was physically cutting me. I also wasn't very good at ignoring it – I'd properly go searching. I'd sit searching on Google for hours and trawl through the mentions of my name. I was so young, and when you're young you just want to be liked. You want to be popular and you get your validation from your peers. Now that peer group was on an insane scale and the feedback could be cruel. It was hard not to listen to it all.

It's only with age that I've stopped being as bothered. I suppose you get to a point where you realise you have your friends and their opinions are the only ones that count. I'm so lucky that I still have the same friends I've had since I was 13. Always having a finger in that pie kept me sane but it also kept me grounded (didn't mean for that to sound so wrong – definitely does). It's funny because people assume *The Inbetweeners* must have changed my life, and in some ways it did, but mostly I just carried on as I always had – living in the arse end of nowhere in Bedfordshire, hanging around with the same bunch of ragtag boys and beautiful girls.

If I've got to a point where I can brush off nasty stories in the press, unfortunately there are still things I find hard to dismiss. No one tells you that fame can actually be isolating. It's fine when you're with your long-term friends who knew you when the only thing you were famous for was your bra size, or at an industry thing when there are other 'celebs' around you. But the rest of the time you're in the real world, being a real person – and the way other real people can treat you ranges a lot. I've been at weddings where I've felt like people could actually see through me because no one will speak to me. I'll go home and see people I used to know from 'the time before' walking down the street, and I'll say hi to them and they'll ignore me; they won't even look me in the eye. You stop being invited to normal stuff because people think you're busy or won't want to come. People talk loudly about how indifferent they are to you *right next to you*. I was at an airport the other day when I heard a group of women talking about me. Some of them were being sweet, saying, 'Oh look, Emily Atack's over there – she's so nice, let's go and say hi.' And then their friends said, 'Oh God, really? Why on earth would you care about saying hi to her, she's so irrelevant. I refuse to watch her in anything.' And my heart crumbled a little bit. Did they know I could hear them? Did they care?

I'm so lucky, please don't think I don't know that. But when you're in any of the above situations, invitations to a new make-up launch or bar opening don't mean anything. Nothing is worse than being ignored, or hearing people choose to ignore you. I think some people think celebrities don't want to be bothered and that's why they stay away. I can't speak for everyone else on TV, but I'm telling you now: if you see me in the street and you would like to come over and have a chat or ask me to take 50 different selfies with you – that's fine! You are officially invited! (Caveat: don't be weird or anything and pull up a chair if I'm having dinner with my family, but normal friendly behaviour is very much welcome.)

Sometimes I feel like Julia Roberts in *Notting Hill*. NOT because I think I look like her (I wish) or am as famous as her – there is a point to the story, I promise! Do you remember the scene where Hugh Grant and his friends all offer up why their lives are the most tragic and therefore they deserve the last brownie? They go round the table and miss out Julia's character, Anna Scott, who is a famous Hollywood actress. She pipes up and says, 'Wait, what about me?' And then lists why being an actress isn't all fun and games – the diets, the paps, the personal maintenance etc. Everyone laughs and says not a chance. But that is sometimes how I genuinely feel, even with my friends who I love to death. There's this idea that everything is rosy in the garden of the public eye, and that even if something categorically shit happens to you that would still allow everyone else to have the last brownie, by being in the rosy garden you are automatically discounted from sympathy. I don't need sympathy all the time; I just need it when everyone else would need it. Everything is relative, whether you're on TV, or work in an office or a hospital or a school or a hairdresser's or a bank. Even if you can afford your own gold-plated chocolate desserts sprinkled with unicorn shit – you too will sometimes deserve that last crusty supermarket brownie.

Fame (Not the Musical)

I think, over the years, fame has sometimes made me more self-conscious, and sometimes made me more resilient, but that overall I'm still exactly the same person I ever was. Because, to quote my doppelganger Julia/Anna, 'The fame thing isn't really real.' In the end, we are all just girls, standing in front of boys, asking them to love us – or to get a round of cocktails in before happy hour finishes.

Moving to London

London was always the dream. When I was little, Mum would take me sometimes when she went to do voiceovers. Then when I was 16, I did some work experience at the same studio, and I remember thinking, 'This is the life.' I wanted to be in a fancy outfit, coffee in one hand, sunglasses down, strolling arm in arm with my friends through the crowds in Soho, watching posh people go by in their flash cars or carrying dogs in their handbags, rolling our eyes at tourists who stood lost in the middle of pavements, heading to trendy bars with the whole of the front window pulled back, the people inside spilling out onto the road with a drink in one hand and a cigarette in the other as the sun went down.

Finally, when I was 24, I made it. It was emotionally traumatising. Not because London's scary – it really isn't – but because it meant leaving Martha behind, and I'd never not lived with her before. She was staying in the flat in Bedfordshire and her boyfriend was moving in, so I knew she'd be looked after, but it still felt wrong. You know that feeling when you accidentally leave your phone at home and you keep going to check it but then you remember you don't have it? That's what it felt like. Like I'd lost a limb.

We packed all my stuff up into a van that my dad was helping me to drive to my new flat, and Martha and I couldn't even look at each other. We couldn't say goodbye; that would have felt too wrong. So we just said, 'Bye, then!' without so much as a hug, and I jumped in the front seat. I've never had to try so hard to fight back my tears – there must have been 92 lumps in my stomach that had been in my throat by the time we got to London.

I was moving in with my lovely friend Craig, who worked in PR and lived in Kentish Town. Dad carried my stuff into the flat with me and then said, 'Great, that's everything. See you later.' I was like, 'Oh no, oh no, oh no', because I was so terrified of being left in this new place by myself (Craig was at work). But *technically* I was an adult, so he didn't have any qualms about leaving me to it.

First things first: I looked in the fridge. Craig had already stocked it with a bottle of prosecco, which made me feel instantly better – empty fridges are BAD OMENS. I looked at the clock and knew that in approximately four hours he would be home and drinking it with me. I used the time to create my nest – it has become apparent to me over the years that when I'm in a new place, I have to immediately fill it with candles, throws, pictures and fairy lights so that I feel safe and contained. A fairy light-lit womb, if you can imagine. By the time Craig, and our other housemate, Abby, came home, I was feeling better. We ate our dinner off cheap camping stuff because we hadn't bought any proper kitchenware yet, drank the prosecco and then polished off a bottle of red wine. Which nicely set the tone for the years that would follow.

The time I spent in that flat is flooded with some of the happiest memories I own. Kentish Town, if you don't know it, is in north-west London, not far from Camden. It's a maze of shabby streets and some that would give Notting Hill a run for its money – ice-cream-coloured houses with smart white windows and flowers in neat pots on the sills. The pubs are epic – best pub crawls a girl could ask for – and there's an amazing music scene. Like most of London, it's both fancy and run-down; you can't swing a cat without hitting a celebrity, but there's also an upsetting number of sleeping bags in doorways that breaks your heart.

Our flat was on one of the last cobbled streets left in London, above a pub called the Assembly House. I love pointing it out to people now – there's a little turret on the top floor and that was where we lived. It wasn't anything to write home about: it was grubby around the edges, always dusty, we forever had mice, and it got wrecked from time to time when people came round and spilt beer on the sofa or in our shoes. But we loved it. You could climb out one of the windows to sit on a little bit of flat roof and look out over the jumble of streets – the view was beautiful, especially when there was a good sunset going.

My memories of it are all sunny. In summer we'd spend lazy days on Hampstead Heath, with picnics and drink all weekend. They were the days before hangovers, when Sunday drinking was the most beautiful thing in the world, especially when accompanied by a roast.

Craig was the perfect person to introduce me to the rest of London because of his job in PR. There were always bar openings to go to, new restaurants to try, and he introduced me to all his friends, some of whom I still see all the time now. I was going out with Jason the whole time I was there (more on this later) – between the odd jobs I was doing and his modelling career, things felt steady and unbreakable. There wasn't a lot of money, but there was enough.

If it sounds like I'm remembering it wearing

rose-tinted glasses, I probably am. I haven't thought about those years much recently because they are tinged with what happened with Jason; I'm so glad this book has reminded me of all the good bits in them! They were such fun years. There's something about London you can't quite put your finger on that makes you feel included, like you're part of the fabric of something bigger. I wasn't getting tons of work, but for the first time I felt like I'd made it, like I was living the life that had always been waiting for me.

The Kentish Town years ended after I moved to Camden with Jason, and although I moved back afterwards, time had shifted on – like it has a pesky habit of doing. Everyone's still game for a laugh, still likes the pub, still goes out, but we're probably a bit more worn-out these days and we can't fight the hangovers, or the grubbiness, like we used to. I live on my own now, which is too grown-up to admit to, but I'm still in north London. If I stop and think about my time here, I can feel the happiness rising up out of the pavements.

Funnily enough, I sometimes go to the place where I did my work experience for my own voice-overs now. Some of the same people work there still and remember me from when I was 16. We have a laugh about how nothing's really changed during that time. I love the familiar nature of Soho. From being a toddler on mum's arm eating Celebrations in a sound-studio's funky reception area to being a proper grown up running around to meetings and castings. Walking down Greek Street on a sunny afternoon, I still feel a flicker of pride in my achievements. I still feel like that 16 year old who was lost, getting coffee during a brief stint of work experience, but now with big sunglasses and a floaty dress on. And the coffee I'm holding is mine.

The People Who Shaped Me: London's Finest

Not all friends stick around for the whole show, but I've found the brief and beautiful ones can have some of the biggest influences on your happiness. Since I came to London I've made some incredible new friends, if only for one night. London churns out a tornado of characters – smoky, boozy, weird and wonderful, just like London itself. You're all friends with the same city and that's a good starting point. I have found myself clicking with someone by the loch in Camden one sunny Saturday after too much warm Pimm's.

People like my friend Joel (we call him 'great-time' Joel) who I met in 'London's smallest cocktail bar' in Kentish Town. A bar fashioned from disused underground toilets, it's tiny, it's fabulous. Martha and I were having a post-work cocktail and debrief about life. Joel, tall, handsome, a big fat Rolex on his wrist started chatting to us. We rolled our eyes, and looked away – weirdo. But he kept on. He asked us what we did, he was determined to get a convo going. I soon realised that he was a Northerner, Manchester – perhaps? He wasn't chatting us up, but just chatting. He worked in the bar trade, we talked about cocktails, we talked about work, he was interesting, he was nice. He joined our table. Martha and Joel got into some heated but hilarious debates about business. He was smiling over his Margarita, listening, laughing through giving his well-crafted opinion. I liked him so much that he's become one of my dearest London friends! We have lunch at the best places in the city, we have rosé at Soho House. He has ALWAYS got a stunningly attractive girlfriend who is too young for him. He comes to my work events and supports me, he was there at my stand-up gig at Clapham in the royal box. I had to laugh. I found a friend in a renovated toilet wearing a Rolex on a Wednesday night and that is why I love London.

London gives you friends like Joel, and friends that you have Sunday roasts with because you want to start drinking again to ease a hangover. It's the ones with black Merlot teeth, who demand a game of Scrabble in the pub, as they hurl the badly worn box down onto the table, only to abandon it ten minutes later. It's the skint ones, the rich ones and the ones who never go to bed. The ones who demand you stay out for one more on a Thursday and before you know it the sun is coming up. It's the PRs who message you, 'Fancy this?' followed by a ridiculous flyer to a party that looks too good to be true. You never actually go; you'd rather stay north and go to the wine bar you've been to 5,000 times. But it's always an exciting reminder that, in London, any time, any day of the week, something wildly tempting is happening around the corner, and it's up to you if you're up for a dip.

You might not know any of these people when you're 45 and living in the arse end of nowhere, but for now they bring you out of your shell and strangely but magically uncover parts of your personality that your best friends hadn't found before. For me, they were like the last elusive puzzle piece that I hadn't noticed was missing from my picture beforehand but suddenly made me feel all the more complete.

Showbiz: The Good, The Bad and The Ugly

The Good

I love acting. I love getting lost in scripts, I love disappearing under make-up and costumes and reappearing as someone else, I love working with great people. It doesn't matter what people chuck at me now when it comes to work, scripted projects are my biggest passion and will always be my preference when it comes to my next job. In 2014, I was in a low-budget film called *Almost Married* – it was about a guy and a girl who are about to tie the knot, but then the guy realises he picked up an STI while on his stag-do. (Critics choice here we come.) For the most part it was just me and two actors: Philip McGinley and Mark Stobbart. It wasn't extravagant or exciting, but we filmed in Newcastle for a month and it was just so fun. We went out every night and ate Japanese food and drank and just had a really good time. Sometimes when things feel a bit messy at home, the freedom of going somewhere different, of spending every waking moment with new people who can bring you out of yourself, is like medicine.

Dad's Army was also an incredible experience. We were filming in Bridlington, which is a picture-postcard town on the Yorkshire coast, and I was working with some of the most amazing people in the industry: Bill Nighy, Toby Jones, Danny Mays, Catherine Zeta-Jones, Michael Gambon, Tom Courtenay – people say never meet your heroes, but I met A LOT of heroes on that job and they were nothing but wonderful and incredible and amazing. The very first film I did, *Outside Bet*, was the same – it was with Bob Hoskins and he was such a gentleman. I remember after my first scene he came up to me and told me he'd been watching it on the monitor. He said to me, 'I hope you've got a fucking good agent.' What a babe.

American jobs are a different kettle of fish. The first American film I did was called *The Hoarder*, with Mischa Barton and Robert Knepper (if you can't place him, he played T-Bag in *Prison Break*). I had a few days off and I couldn't believe it but the team behind the movie agreed to fly Martha out to meet me. The shoot was in New York, so basically this meant Martha and I had six days to piss about

Manhattan together pretending we were from *Sex and the City*. When you're on a film shoot you get given something called per diems – it's an allowance per day to be spent on food and any necessities you need, normally it's about 100 quid. This time it was about 600 dollars as it was a much higher budget movie. Martha touched down at JFK, we nipped back to the Soho Grand (google it, it's epic) to spruce up, then went to a restaurant and lounge called STK and spent *all* my per diems on the first night. It was a FANTASTIC night. And a fantastic six days, truth be told – just imagine Martha and me strolling around Central Park with a bottle of wine each and you'll have a pretty good picture of what happened.

The Bad

The hilarious thing about acting is that everybody thinks it's the most glamorous thing ever, but for the majority of the time it really isn't at all – stories like the one I just gave you are very rare. Here's a day in the life of being an actor for you:

Eat crisps and stare at the ceiling.

Ha – just kidding. Although, when you're not working, genuinely you spend a lot of your time hating on the fact your friends all have nine-to-five jobs as no one's around.

But when you're on a job, it's all go: 5am you wake up in some kind of hotel. Sometimes they're nice, sometimes they're shit. A friendly driver comes to pick you up and you get whisked to the least Hollywood place ever: a trailer park full of, you guessed it, trailers and (my favourite) a catering truck. Most of the things I've shot for have been made in winter, so it's still dark outside and bloody cold. You go into your little trailer, which is effectively a freezer, and then a lovely runner comes to take your order for breakfast. I always go all-out and think, 'Well, I'm working so I'm actually allowed three hash browns, four sausages, five bits of bacon, nine bits of toast.' And then I sit there stuffing my face, dribble of ketchup running down my chin, while my poor make-up artist tries to do something to me.

Hair and make-up done, you get into your costume (which for me was not always season appropriate so you shiver some more) and wait for something to happen. Usually it's a good two hours. Normal people probably catch up on emails and get their laptop out, but I just sit and listen to music. If I'm still sleepy I'll put on some country and pretend I'm in a music video. Marvellous.

And then eventually you get called to set. You stand around with your hands stuffed inside your North Face coat for another hour while they're lighting up and rigging, having a chat with whoever's knocking about. You do about ten minutes of a scene. You go back to your trailer for another three hours. You come back. You do another tiny bit. And then you're done! You wrap at about seven o'clock, go back to your hotel, get a bit of room service, drink a bottle of red wine. Or you go into the bar and have a bottle of red wine with the crew and the cast members, have a few cheeky flirts with the actors. See which ones are single and out of those who you want to cop off with. (I'm kidding. Sort of.) And then you go to bed. Oh, the glamour!

I remember once on *Dad's Army*, we were all huddled in this freezing-cold trailer – Bill Nighy, Toby Jones, Michael Gambon, Tom Courtenay, Alison Steadman – eating out of these plastic lunch-boxes with plastic forks, the building literally falling apart around us. Toby Jones once had a screw plop right in his food from the ceiling above. We were all laughing hysterically because it was such a classic example of life as an actor. Cor, it's glorious, but it's definitely not glamorous.

The Ugly

I'd say 90 per cent of the projects I've worked on have been wonderful experiences. I've nearly always had directors and men treating me with nothing but respect and I'm so lucky for that. But there have been a couple of occasions that really were not okay, and it made me understand that women in this business have had to put up with bad, awful, behaviour for far too long.

There was one person I worked with – let's call him Frank – who said a string of really inappropriate things to me and then started sending me texts. The comments started with little things. I think he saw that I'm a very chatty person. I think if you're quite fun and full of energy people just want to be your pal at first, but he was older than me, lots older. 'You haven't given me a hug today. You've hugged all the other boys, why haven't you given me a hug?' All in a silly little, almost baby-like voice. I brushed it off but then he started saying slightly more crude things to me when people weren't in earshot.

And then we were doing a take where I was 'shock horror', having to play 'sexy'. I was required to bend down, I think they were after a sexy arse shot. Again, shock horror. We'd done the first take of it but then he came over and whispered something truly sexually inappropriate in my ear. I began to freeze up. I felt like my heart was slowing to a stop. 'Oh my God,' I thought, 'this has gone too far.'

Luckily one of the make-up girls actually heard and sort of whacked him on the arm and said, 'Frank, you can't say that!', and I could see the embarrassment in his face, because he'd been overheard, and he went bright red and just laughed it off.

'Oh, she knows I'm only kidding,' he said.

A day or so later, I was in the front of the car. We were all travelling back to the hotel and he started sending me texts from the back of the car: 'You haven't spoken to me much today.' Things like that, texts that out of context sound innocent but all together were unsettling and made me feel really uncomfortable. It was so weird because there was never any point where I gave him any kind of inkling that I was remotely sexually interested in him.

These little texts continued and I started to panic because he was going to be on my next job. There was a chance that this next job could shoot in the US and I of course was really looking forward to it. 'I'm gonna make sure our hotel rooms are really close together in America so we can go for dinner and stuff and have fun,' he would say.

I remember thinking to myself, 'Oh my God, he's going to be fucking knocking at my door every night.' I felt really uncomfortable about it and it made me dread this trip.

The volume of comments was getting more and more and so I just started to be really stand-offish with him. I thought, 'I can't be smiley.' Before, I'd blush – because I was genuinely embarrassed – and just try to laugh it off, but that hadn't worked, so I tried the cold shoulder route instead. He got more and more arsey with me because I wasn't responding to his advances

The shoot ended and, a fortnight later, all over the press were pictures of another actress in my role. I never received an explanation about why I'd been dropped; just one minute I'm doing it and I'm all excited to go, and the next thing I know there's another actress doing it. Sometimes stuff like that happens, it just wasn't meant to be.

Sometimes I think about how I might react to Frank now, would I stand firm? Tell him to fuck off? I'd like to think that now I would call someone out on such behaviour. Perhaps I would try a polite but firm, 'Don't say that to me, please.' Rightly or wrongly, I always thought about all the other people involved if you *did* speak up. It's hard if they're married with children, which they quite often are, because you think,

'I can't ruin this family. It's gonna destroy those kids' lives if they hear this about their dad.' Or the wife would be devastated. They may be a complete creep but I will hurt a whole load of innocent people if I say something. That's my personal thing. A lot of people won't agree with me on that and I completely understand. One less creep at work is another one we have beaten, no matter how minor their actions. But with that particular situation, I processed my thoughts and assessed the impact it had on me. I'm not scarred for life by it. I'm fine. Yes, it's shitty and horrible, but I'm okay. He knows what he was doing was inappropriate. He must do. He can live with that now.

As well as the impact on others, I think of myself. I never would have felt able to stand up to anyone in senior positions as a young actress, because they have all the power professionally. When I was younger, I needed all the work that I could get. This was a time when I was on a roll, getting more and more work and things were really looking up. The last thing I was going to do was put a huge spanner in the works. In effect, you don't really feel like you have the choice to do anything about it.

The one other occasion where I felt powerless to stop something was with a guy on the set of another project – let's call him Dave. There was a group of us on set, all around a similar age, talking about sex. I was being vocal in the discussion – I can talk about sex until the cows come home if I'm in an environment where everyone's comfortable with that. Dave was quite a lot older, and he must have heard this conversation. Because then he started talking to me about that kind of stuff, but not in a group situation – when it was just the two of us. I made it very clear that I wasn't going to talk to him about that kind of thing, now that the group chat was over. He tried it a couple more times, sort of quietly passing the odd naughty comment here and there. I ignored it. I stood firm.

But then one day I was filming a sex scene and Dave was there. Afterwards, I was walking to get some lunch on my own when he came up behind me and put a condom in my pocket and said to me, 'Let's go somewhere right now.' My heart just went into my throat. Out of a mix of shock and horror, I nervously laughed it off. 'Don't be silly,' I tried. 'What do you mean? I'm going for lunch.'

'Come on, let's go somewhere,' he said again, pulling on my hand. I had to really put my foot down and say, 'Absolutely not. That's ludicrous.' I got away from him as per the time before and just tried to block that out of my mind.

The night of the wrap party came round and we

were all drinking in the hotel. I was drunk. I wasn't single. I was with someone at the time, so I had no intention of doing anything with anybody. I was just having fun, letting my hair down, messing around with the cast I'd got to know really well. We were stumbling around the hotel corridors when we ran out of wine, so I asked if anyone had any left in their room, because we'd all been given a bottle or two. One of the group gave me a key and told me there was a mini fridge of booze in their room. I said, 'Great', took the key and went to the room. Opened the door, walked over to the fridge, opened it – no booze in there. And all of a sudden I turned round and Dave is standing there, in the room with his dick out.

I froze. I remember saying, drunkenly, 'No,' but I didn't have a clue what to do. I was drunk, for one, but not so drunk that I couldn't realise this was a really fucking tense situation. I asked him to let me out of the room and he said, 'I'll only go if you give me something.'

So then I kissed him. I just snogged him for a few seconds. Felt sick the entire time but I knew that was the only way I was going to get out of the room. He let me leave and the next day I cried my eyes out all day. It's always emotional after wrap parties, and of course there's also the hangover paranoia. But it was also because of what had happened with that man. *It's because I'm loud and silly and I get too drunk and I'm flirtatious with all the other boys. I dance provocatively. It was my fault.* As far as I was concerned, it was totally my fault.

I called Martha and told her all about it. She said, 'This shouldn't be happening to you.' She said, 'What do we do about this? We need to say something.'

I said we couldn't. We cannot say anything to anyone ever. I just wanted to forget that it had happened. Perhaps that makes me weak, I don't know. This is the first time I've recalled it to anyone other than Martha.

I'd love to say that with age, courage and experience, if it happened now, I'd kick him in the balls and leg it out of there as fast as I could. But I realise that for any woman (or man) who has found themselves in a situation like this, you just don't know how you'll react, or the impact it has after. But when you're drunk, standing in a room with a man who holds more power than you, instinct takes over, to get you the hell out of there. Whatever it takes.

I've read with horror about the stories from women around the world, from brief encounters with men at work to violent stories about something far more sinister. I've been amazed by the bravery of the women speaking out and sharing their stories – and I also stand with those who perhaps still aren't ready to as well.

The People
Who Shaped
Me: Team Atack

Everyone else I've included in these spotlights have been friends or family, who gradually over the years have taken me and moulded me like a lump of clay into the Emily you see now. But then there are the people who literally keep you in one piece from day to day and who never get enough credit for being the gods of your life. Let me tell you now, the people in showbiz do not get anywhere on their own – they all have brilliant teams standing behind them. Celebrities are a bit like dogs: they come in different shapes and sizes, they're mostly cuddly (you get the odd Rottweiler and annoying yappy one), and people like to watch them scampering around. Meanwhile, their team are like their humans, ferrying them from place to place, looking after them and, more often than not, walking behind carrying the poo bag.

My team is the best in the business and a big part of it is my primary agent, Alex, who knows the truth, the whole truth and nothing but the truth. Alex has seen me at my worst, my best and everything in between; he has championed me in this industry when nobody wanted to know. He knocked on doors, pushed and believed in me when I didn't believe in myself. He's made decisions for me that have guided me down the right path when I couldn't see the signs. He's helped me carve a steady 12-year career out of an industry where nothing is certain. He is constant and he is dedicated. The man is a machine. He's also like my brother – the poor lad was woken up by me banging on his door at 3am one night in LA, too drunk to find my room. We've chatted non-stop on long-haul flights and for hours on the phone. He has seen me trying to stuff myself into a BAFTA dress so tight that I thought it might kill me. Even when I've been exploding out of a corset with my granny pants on he tells me I look lovely. He's not a wheeler-dealer manager; he trained under one of the best agents in the world and it shows. I trust him completely.

I also have to give a big shout-out to my afore-mentioned cousin, Lydia, my make-up artist. She is the only person I trust to make up this big old head and she deserves to add 10 per cent client counselling tax to her invoice and to win a Pride of Britain award for the amount she has to deal with. Make-up artists are fascinating cogs in the system. They have to be present, yet invisible. Have authority, yet be malleable. In fact, I think out of all of the jobs on a TV set or photoshoot they have it roughest – imagine having to get up close and personal with someone's face you've never met or do a slightly scary celeb's hair. It must be arse-sweatingly stressful.

Everyone loves Lydia. She glides around a set with her kit bag on hip, a brush between each finger. I am so familiar with the sight of her face close to mine, with her glasses on the end of her nose as she dabs and probes and tweaks my face. She created my jungle-inspired crimped-hair look that has become my absolute go-to and always makes me feel fabulous.

Alex, Lydia and all the rest of the management crew (including Martha, but if I give her any more shout-outs her head's going to get too big for her body) have stuck by me through the good times and the bad. I don't know where I'd be without them.

The Elephant
in the Room

Food has always been a big part of my life. Whether it's in my aunty's kitchen or around tables pushed together in a restaurant, eating is how we get together as a family, it's what our holidays revolved around when we were younger and still do now. Indian is our go-to for any problem; there's nothing you can't face or beat if you've got a rogan josh and saag aloo in front of you. Food to me means togetherness and cosiness. It means an occasion. And I love that.

But loving food can be tricky when you're in an image-driven business, and even if you're not, it's stating the obvious to say there is an accepted form of beauty that we're all sort of conditioned to want to be from a very early age – as soon as we're old enough to watch adverts on the TV and see women on the sides of buses. I was definitely conscious of my weight from a very young age, I think maybe because I've always been quite physically aware of myself in general. It probably sounds vain but I'm sure it's true for lots of little girls: I wanted to be pretty and thin and look like Britney Spears in the 'Hit Me Baby One More Time' video. I was always quite slim growing up – I never seemed to go through a chubby stage like my brother and sister did (sorry guys). And I always had a really healthy relationship with food. I was always keen to try new things and I wasn't fussy. Which meant, unlike lots of kids, I wasn't bothered about chicken nuggets and chips. I mean, sure, I loved a McDonald's as a treat, or when my mum couldn't be arsed to cook, but I never had that fussiness of only wanting crappy fast and sugary food. In all things, I was desperate to be an adult and food was no exception: I liked seafood, and the sophisticated pasta dishes my dad would cook. While kids were snacking on bread and ice cream on holidays, I'd be asking my mum and dad to buy me some rollmop herrings like a little weirdo, and diving headfirst into the paella at lunchtime. So even though I ate a lot, I ate quite healthily for a kid.

By the time I was about ten or 11, I had started my periods and I grew boobs. I had big old boobies by 12 and was known as Boobzilla in my year at school. (Weirdly, I took Boobzilla as a compliment.) Because I'd hit puberty at a young age, my body became curvy and womanly pretty quickly. I was also quite tall. I'm a fairly average height of five-six now but the growth spurts that got me there happened not too long after I'd got my period, so at 13 I was a head above most of the other people in my year. So, because there was a marked difference in the way I looked compared to other girls my age, I was always very aware of my appearance. Once teenagedom hit, my parents' friends started to comment on how much I'd changed. 'My God, hasn't she grown up! She's like a model!' – that sort of thing. Their reactions made me start to kind of believe that I really did look quite different to most of my peers. I also wore a lot of make-up, which was rarer for young girls back then. I remember being the only girl I knew who was contouring and drawing on extra-thick lips at 12 years old.

Wearing lots of make-up, by the way, wasn't because I was insecure about my face and looks. After *I'm a Celeb* ... I had a few people being very lovely to me and telling me that I should ditch all the make-up and 'unleash all my beautiful freckles'. Before the jungle I would never have gone down the street with a naked face, I do sometimes do it now and actually feel much more confident about it. But in truth, wearing make-up for me is actually a part of my identity. I'm not ashamed to love it. When I was little, I loved watching my grandma and my mum at their dressing tables and so, as soon as I was old enough to have my own powder set and mascara, it felt like the most natural thing in the world. I love make-up – the feel of it on my skin, the perfume of it, the versatility of it. Putting foundation on isn't about hiding my face, it's more like putting on my armour, to tackle the day. I feel powerful when I'm made up. I feel like me.

By 15, 16 I dropped quite a lot of weight because I was stressed and lovesick all the time, and instead of eating I was smoking and drinking in parks with my friends. But then at 17, once I was happier in myself again, I all of a sudden gained quite a lot. I had discovered wine, and getting takeaways with my nice new boyfriend Daniel. Seeing myself on TV for the first time I got a shock. I thought 'the camera adds ten pounds' was just a saying, but it really isn't. It's completely true. And once I had seen myself on TV, I knew from then on my weight was always going to be a complex subject in my life.

The more I worked in TV, the more I realised I was on the larger side compared to most actresses. When I played Charlotte Hinchcliffe in *The Inbetweeners*, it was the first time I had ever heard negative comments about my weight. I was one of the first girls on TV to be playing a sexy girl-next-door type, who wasn't a size 6. I was a size 10/12, but to people who were watching I was plus size, or chubby, or overweight. I guess because nobody was used to seeing this type of character played by a girl above a size 6 or 8. Social media back then wasn't as big as it is now, but I became obsessed with googling my name and searching forums where people were talking about *The Inbetweeners*, just so I could see if people were saying anything about me and my weight. Some people said horrendous things, some people said nice things like, 'Well I think she's a normal and healthy-looking girl which is a better role model to have for young girls!' But that hurt too because I wanted to be seen as thin. I wanted to be like every other actress and look the same as all the girls in the casting rooms when I went to auditions. I was always the biggest girl in there and I hated it. I felt like a big fat ogre towering above all these tiny, gorgeous, dinky little actresses, so I started trying to diet and working out with a personal trainer. By 18, 19 I was much fitter (and by fitter, I mean drinking vodka Diet Cokes instead of wine). And I made healthier eating choices (and by healthier, I mean ordering a salad with a side of chips). Looking back at photos around this time I can't believe how good I looked, and yet I still felt big, still felt like the odd one out at castings. Because

I was. It was the elephant in the room. Literally. Casting directors and people in the business would hint at me to lose weight, although it wasn't stopping me from getting sexy parts in films, and I was actually on a bit of a roll. But even when I was getting those parts, I still felt like my image wasn't good enough, and I wasn't thin enough.

Dancing on Ice came along when I was 19, which made the weight fall off me. Looking back, I was tiny – I was nine stone and had a full-on lollypop head. And yet I was still being referred to as the curvy girl. Around that time, I was in discussions with LA managers to make my first visit to the city. I remember Skyping one woman, who wanted me to fly over to meet her with a view to potentially signing me. I asked her when she thought it would be a good time to come and she said, 'Well, Emily, to be honest ... we aren't even going to think about getting you over here until you are at least a size 2.' Her EXACT words. I hung up the call and made an internal, conscious decision to knock LA on the head as I knew I was never, ever going to be whatever it was they wanted me to be. I plucked up the courage and told my English agents that I just didn't think Hollywood was a path I could go down at that moment in time.

The Elephant in the Room

As I've gone through my twenties my weight has been up and down. There are times where I've gone a bit silly on the wine and the dinners out with my friends, takeaways, dinner parties and so on. When I've noticed I've gained a fair bit, I rejoin a gym, cut down on the booze and go healthy for a while. I am more than happy to accept that I am on the telly and therefore it is part of my job to think about maintaining a healthy image. And it's also important for my own self-esteem that I'm happy with how I look when I watch myself back, not to mention that eating well and getting fit is good for your mental health. But nowadays I never diet. I never starve myself; I never deprive myself of the things that bring me so much joy in my life. Because I don't believe that is the answer. I love my job, and I love that I've had the opportunities to play glamorous and sexy roles, and posed for *FHM*, and have had people tell me that I'm pretty. It's really lovely and flattering, and I am proud of all those things. But I came to the conclusion quite a long time ago that I will never be that person who starves herself for her job. I make sacrifices for my job in other ways, but sacrificing paella on the beach with gallons of white wine, pizza with my mates, roast dinners on a Sunday, and my dad's giant bowls of pasta ...

that is something I will never, ever deprive myself of. Because those things bring me happiness, way more happiness than a thigh gap ever could.

It's hard sometimes to find your place in the industry I am in, and it's even harder maintaining your place there once you've found it. My problem was I never really knew where I fitted. I was an *inbetweener*, I guess! Not skinny enough for the A-list beautiful leading-lady parts, yet not big enough to play the large funny girl. As the years passed, it made me think more and more about how I wanted to be defined and whether there was anything I could do to turn who I was – not thin enough, not fat enough – into an advantage. As a woman in the entertainment world, you do also have to be realistic about the fact that it can be a bit cruel as you get older. My boobs are getting saggier now, my arse isn't getting rounder sadly but flatter (ha!) and I can't play sexy schoolgirls anymore. But my personality – that's not going anywhere. So I thought: what if I could put myself out there and see what people think of my personality rather than just my weight, or my boobs, or my hilariously misinformed sex appeal? I am a good and kind person, and I like making people laugh. Maybe I should try to do that for a bit and see how it goes? Maybe people will be pleasantly surprised that I really am NOT what it says on the tin. That there's more to me than just the tits and teeth, and that I have a story to tell? Then the jungle came knocking. It was perfect timing.

There will always be times in my life when I feel crap about my weight, and then there will be times I'm feeling good. And I'm never going to be able to completely cut out making comparisons – we're all human, and we can't help but look at other people and sometimes want what they've got. There will always be someone on the beach who has a body I would kill to have, or someone who puts up a load of gym selfies on Instagram while I'm dying of a hangover in bed at ten in the morning, wishing I hadn't drunk all the wine in Soho and eaten two burgers at 4am in Balans on Old Compton Street. But actually, I'm getting to a point in my life where I can look at those beautiful bodies and think to myself, 'Good on them.' If that's what they want to put their energy into, that's great. Personally, I'd rather have the pizza.

I will still sometimes be the largest girl in the casting room when auditioning for a job. But the difference now is that I am fine with that. I am no longer apologising for who I am, because I've learnt that people like me for me. Being in the jungle allowed me to come out and show the country who I was as a person, and I am really lucky that most people didn't just think I was a twat.

I will continue to love my job, and work hard. At the moment, I'm working harder than I ever have before. But as me. And if anything ever requires me to be anything but myself ... I would rather be the elephant in the room.

Five Foods to Take on a Desert Island

1. Assorted flavoured crisps with various dips. I find that no matter what, I am always in the mood for crisps and dip. I tend to go for Walkers Sensations Thai sweet chilli flavour with a caramelised onion humous. Crisps in a bowl and dip never fails to make me feel cosy and like I've created a fun little vibe for myself. And, let's face it, being on a desert island would be pretty boring after a while so you'd need to create a mini vibe. This combo is also perfect at any time of the day when you fancy a snack (though NOT before midday – crisps for breakfast is a bit depressing).

2. Eggs and avocados. You cannot go wrong with a show-off poached egg and avo for brekky. Providing that you've got the fire going like a legend on this island, eggs would go a long way. Fried, scrambled, poached or boiled – they're so efficient cos there's so much use you could get out of them. I would have eggs and avo every morning if I could be arsed – and on an island I would definitely be arsed cos there's bugger all else to do.

3.   Rice. I learnt in the jungle that rice is a lifesaver. I'd take loads of rice, then go and catch loads of fish, crabs, lobsters, mussels, clams etc. from the sea and make an amazing seafood stir-fry with paella rice. I'd obviously have to learn how to catch stuff with a big spike, like Tom Hanks does in *Cast Away*. This would be great for lunch and fill me up for most of the day, and I'd feel like I was on holiday in Spain with my family. I'd probably end up feeling too guilty about killing the little fishies, though, so I'd wind up sacking that off and be left with plain rice.

4.   Burgers with buns. I'd get those burgers on the go for dinner on my massive fire that I've started all by myself. And I'd have made some kind of fruity chutney sauce by now from all the fruit I've found and collected on the island (I'm imagining an island where it's very tropical and there's lots of colourful fruits knocking about), so that would go nicely on the burgers. (In the normal world I'd have sweet potato fries with the burg, but we're on an island and I can't think how I'd cook the sweet potatoes – let's be realistic.)

5.   A cheese board. Obviously. Various different cheeses and biscuits. I'd have this at night-time

before getting into my little desert island hammock. It would make me think of Christmas at my aunty Amy's, where every year I demolish at least an entire wheel of brie by myself. The fruity chutney I've made (see above) goes perfectly with it, and I can also use the cheese for the burgers. It's perfect. I could even crush up the biscuits to make some kind of crumble and use the fun, sexy island fruit to make a dessert! Too far ...?

'Jason'

Of all the loves of my life so far, this is probably the hardest one I will have to write about.

It was 2010, not long after I'd come through my break-up with Daniel, and shortly after the *Dancing on Ice* madness had calmed down. I was approaching 21 and having fun being single, and had no intention of meeting someone serious for a long time. I was enjoying the single life of secret dinner dates, naughty late-night visits to hotels, and cracking on with a few people off the tele who would take you back to their £10 million mansions, show you a nice time and then in the morning their maid (yes this happened) would make you scrambled eggs before you hid under a coat and made a dash for a taxi that was taking you back to your very normal flat in Bedfordshire. 'WHAT IS MY LIFE?!' I would think, giggling to myself all the way back.

By the time I met Jason, I was having fun with one particularly famous boy: we were BBming each other and making long late-night phone calls (you know the ones – the type where you're a bit embarrassed afterwards about what you said). There were topless roll-arounds in various massive houses with various boys with massive personalities. I'd wake up in places like Fulham with my false eyelashes still stuck on my face, desperately searching for a glass for water.

I was in Milton Keynes shopping centre with my cousin Lydia and our friend Carl. Lydia grabbed my arm and said, 'Wow, look at this guy about to walk past Topshop.' I turned and honestly couldn't believe my eyes. A six-foot, brown-eyed, curly-haired boy was walking past. I had honestly never seen anyone so handsome. He looked like an actual Disney prince. Chiselled jaw, pouty lips, in Hollister shorts, t-shirt and flip-flops, tanned and completely perfect. I don't know if I believe in love at first sight but it's the closest I've ever come. I quite literally stood there and said to Lydia, 'Oh my good God. I need him to be my boyfriend.'

I started to sneakily follow him (yep, honestly). He went into a cool surfer type shop and then I realised that he worked there. I quickly formulated a plan. Try and get me to the post office to collect my undelivered parcels is an impossible task but watch me hatch a plan to track down a Disney Prince. I'd come back to the shopping centre the next day, go up to my friend Zach who also worked there, and get him to introduce me.

I strolled into the store the next day, sauntered casually up to Zach, making out I'd only come in to see him, then said, 'Right, the lad with the curly brown hair who works here. What's his name?' Zach laughed and knew straight away I was talking about Jason. Apparently, lots of people asked. Jason, it turned out, had only just turned 18. Christ. I was a cougar at 21. Zach introduced us and, that evening, we did the whole adding on Facebook thing and started flirting immediately. He said 'ha' after everything, which kept reminding me of his age, "Yeah I work there. Ha." "Yeah was so lovely to meet you too! Ha!".

But I looked past it. He was too fit.

After a couple of weeks of sitting by my phone waiting for him to text, belly-aching about how long to wait until texting back, wanting to fly into a pile of unicorns when he texted me first, I went out with my cousin Kate to Revs in Milton Keynes one Saturday night. Read: where I knew he'd be hanging out. We ended up snogging all night. It was glorious.

I started to meet him on his lunch breaks, which is where we were papped together for the first time. I was still a bit oblivious to the paps at that point, I certainly didn't expect them to come to Centre

MK! There was interest in who Jason was – he was very new to it all and it freaked him out a bit. So we started hanging out at my flat a lot instead. It was summer, and we spent most evenings walking around parks, sitting by rivers, then gazing at each other in bed till about 5am. I was arse over tit in love with him very quickly. He was so precious and gorgeous and I felt like I wanted to look after him and sort of show him the way a bit. I was his first serious girlfriend, so I was indulging in the maturity of that and how grown-up it made me feel. I liked the fact that I took the reins, I was the experienced one, the one in control for a change, and he hung on every word I said as though it was gospel. Even if I was slightly making it up every now and then. That was very new to me too. But it worked for us. He was my real-life Disney prince and that's genuinely what I called him to his face.

The thing with going out with a real-life Disney prince is that there are a lot of Tinker Bells flying around, extremely green with envy and cross that you are his Wendy. Hovering around with their blonde topknots, trying to sprinkle their fairy dust all over him, fluttering their wings and bending over with their extremely short dresses on and revealing their stunning tiny, toned and tanned bums (Tinker

Bell ALWAYS did that, didn't she?! Little madam).
And it was hard because, well … I was jealous. All
the time. Over every single girl that ever spoke to
him. He was 18 years old and extremely popular. He
knew everyone, especially all the young and utterly
breathtakingly beautiful girls he knew at Hollister
and beyond. I had it in my head that every single
one of them fancied him and I hated it. I was always
friendly to them when I met them – I am certainly
not that horrible girl who scowls at other girls for
no reason. Never have been. I even became quite
pally with a couple of them. But it did make me
feel insecure. It made me feel old and fat and not
as cool as they all were. I also knew that Jason was
so young and new to relationships that I was always
scared his head would turn, or he would test the
boundaries. I had doubt. And I hadn't had that
with Daniel, so it made me panic. I felt like a little
girl again, terrified about my dad running off with
another woman and leaving my mum.

Jason had an amazing family that he was living
with who I became close to very quickly. They lived
about half an hour from my flat and I was spending
most weekends at their house in the countryside. His
lovely mum, his stepdad, gorgeous younger sister
(about 15 when I met her) and a hilarious younger

brother (around seven when I met him) – together we became like a little gang, like I'd had with my family when we were younger, I guess. They lived in a beautiful big house, big garden, huge fridge always full of fun stuff (mainly wine for his mum, stepdad and me to drink). His grandparents also visited a lot and I became really close to his grandma. We'd sit and drink prosecco in the garden and gossip about EVERYTHING.

I spent summers in their garden, drinking with their neighbours, having takeaways, taking their dog Marley for a walk (although I moaned about that bit – wish I hadn't now). Watching Jason and his little brother play football in the garden while I sat and painted (it sounds so fucking middle class when I write it down). I spent winters there putting up Christmas trees, playing chess with his little brother, playing cards with Jason on the sofa, laughing in the kitchen with his sister about ridiculous things. I adored his family as though they were my own. That house made me feel safe and stable. They treated me like a member of the family, and I will always have so much love in my heart for them.

Jason and I had a loving, fun and close relationship. But there were occasional bumps along the way when it came to girls, sometimes with my silly jealousy, but also sometimes because he did give me reasons to feel that way. He was so young, and I truly believed he tried his best to be the man I was trying to mould him into. I struggled with our age gap every now and then because it would show when it came to things like friends and family. I spent a lot of time with his, whereas he didn't take much interest in mine. I would also try to take him with me to friends' parties, or weddings, and he always had an excuse as to why he couldn't come. He would rather play on the PlayStation or go and play football with his friends when I needed picking up from an airport – this was always the sort of stuff we'd clash over. It wasn't his fault; he just wasn't in the same place as I was a lot of the time and that was simply because of our age difference. I know he adored me, but he just didn't quite understand the priorities and the security that I needed. I'd battle with this a lot, but because, overall, we shared so much and we loved each other so much, I just accepted it most of the time. I didn't want to lose him simply because he chose the PlayStation over my best friend's birthday.

When I moved to Kentish Town, Jason began spending more and more time with me there so he eventually moved in. Craig's boyfriend Macgowan then moved in and we were a fun little four. We'd have our ups and downs but we were enjoying living together. Jason had become a model by then and was getting quite regular work, as was I with a few bits to keep me going. We were good. Life was good. We'd spend the week in London, then lots of weekends at his family's house. We'd sing Justin Bieber songs the whole way there and back in Jason's car, bicker about something, fall silent for a moment, then one of us would burst out laughing and the argument would be over. I loved him. I really, really loved him, and he loved me. I could never be angry at him for long. All he had to do was give me a certain smile and I would absolutely forgive anything. It was sometimes like a mother and son irritation! That sounds fucking gross, but what I mean is that I never felt he was doing any wrong as such. He was just a cheeky little shit sometimes and knew he'd get away with it if he cuddled me a certain way or gave me his white, toothy Prince Eric smile. (That's Prince Eric from *The Little Mermaid*, if you didn't catch the reference. I won't be able to listen to the song 'Part of Your World' ever again without thinking of him.) Until one day, unfortunately, something happened that I was unable to quite forgive, and so we 'went on a break'.

In this break, I went away on a work trip with my mum. She was directing a play out of town that was running for a few nights and persuaded me to go with her thinking it would cheer me up. I was heartbroken. Utterly miserable. After the show, I was sat in the bar with some of mum's friends, and actually started to have a good time. A boy came in and joined the group. There was an immediate spark, an immediate attraction, and we started laughing and having fun straight away. I spent the weekend meeting up with him and we established a really great connection. He was older, hilarious, and we were just so similar. I went back to London. We carried on speaking for a little while and then that dried up. I didn't think much else of it other than that I'd had fun over a weekend with someone who made me feel better about my break-up.

Jason then got wind I'd met someone while I had been away and was devastated, to the point where I got a car at three in the morning to go and comfort him and we ended up getting back together. I still loved him. We wanted to fight for our relationship.

After long conversations and making new promises to each other, we moved into a flat together on our own in Camden. It sounds mad when we'd only just got back together, but you know what it's like when you're trying to fix things. We thought creating our own little home together with pictures of us both on the walls, and having dinner parties with our friends, would sort everything. And it does for a while. I'm sure lots of girls can relate to this period of time during relationships that have been through the mill. You nearly lose each other, you come back together, the sex becomes exciting and adventurous again, the flowers and surprise dinners happen again, the late nights of chatting come back, the sacrifices you make become more apparent, and you speak in a nicer and more amicable tone to each other. 'No, of course – you do that tonight, that's totally fine, babe! Enjoy yourself!' And your voices have gone up three keys higher because you're being super-lovely to one another.

While this was all happening, though ... there was still a doubt niggling away, far in the back of my mind. I completely pushed it out and shoved it in a scary-thought drawer because I had to make this work. I was terrified of losing my fairy-tale prince again. But I just couldn't help but think I had already lost something that I couldn't get back. Trust, maybe. Something had gone.

'Jason'

I got a late-night message one night from the man I met on the trip with mum. We started chatting quite a lot. Absolutely nothing bad. The conversations honestly went from sending songs to each other by the band we both liked, to our favourite sandwiches. It was friendly, fun chat, but obviously because of the weekend we had spent together, I knew what I was doing was a little bit naughty. But he made me laugh, we made each other laugh, and we understood each other.

The weeks ticked by, I was on a downward spiral. Jason and I were growing further and further apart. I would lie in bed sobbing silently while he slept next to me, because I knew it was over but I just didn't know how to articulate anything. And the thought of not having Jason in my life was still too painful to fathom. I was heartbroken that since getting back together, I just couldn't get back what we had before. I still loved him so much. I still loved the smell of his neck, his clothes; still looked at him and thought he was the most gorgeous boy in the world. But it was too little too late. I don't know what you call this kind of end to a relationship, really. I have been dumped before but there was something hugely traumatic involved in this kind of ending, it was just closing down, it was the end of the road, for no real reason. I didn't understand. So, one day, I plucked up the courage to tell Jason I wasn't happy.

I was lying in bed waiting for him to come to bed too. I was crying when he came in, and I just said the words, 'I'm unhappy.' Simple as that. They just spilled out of me. I can't really remember what was said, apart from teary words of regret and sadness and reminiscing. We were both heartbroken. We knew deep down it was the right thing, but it's just so fucking hard. When you're breaking up with someone, it's like you're about to die and your love flashes before your eyes. Your love with that person, all your memories, from the second you met to now, all in chronological order, completely flash through your mind as though death is about to take you. And I guess a part of you does die. That's how it feels anyway. My love flashed before my eyes, and it was gone.

We agreed to move out of the flat but still had a month left on the lease, so we were still living together for those few weeks. We were still being nice and kind to each other, cuddling at night-time, crying; I still stroked his hair. And we helped each other with living arrangements. I was going back to the Kentish Town flat and he was moving to a flat-share. I'd been seeing a therapist for the last few months and I was by now on very strong antidepressants. My drinking was bad, my sadness unravelling. And I was slowly going down a very sad and dark path of self-destruction. If I wanted to end my relationship with Jason, I had to do it with a clearer head. So any late night texting, any potential meet ups with rebound men or men that lingered on the outer rings of my life that I knew would pop up at any given moment were off limits. So that was over, my relationship was over, and I felt empty.

Jason and I said our goodbyes and I moved the last of my boxes back into the Kentish Town flat. I knew this really was it, no going back. I kept thinking, 'How can this be the right thing if it hurts this much?'

One day I went out and drank so much that I came home, fell and hit my head on the side of the bath and knocked myself out. My flatmate, Alex, who had also just moved in, found me on the floor and called my parents. Enough was enough and they came to see me.

I was a mess. So, so, so, so, sad. Heartbroken. Questioning everything. Was it all my fault? Probably. I always seem to blame myself for these kinds of things. Maybe if I wasn't so this and so that, blah blah.

With a bit more distance I can see that the fact of the matter was the relationship had run its course. But where does that leave you? Why does that happen? When you have nothing more to pin it on but a simple 'dead end' sign. It's like the end of the film *The Truman Show*, when the boat crashes into the set at the edge of the horizon. Nowhere further to go. But I don't regret trying again. Sometimes you have to go back to really realise. That final go at things gave me consolation that what we had was gone.

Jason has moved on and I'm happy for him. We don't have contact anymore. I think sometimes that's just the way it has to be. It doesn't mean I don't think about him and our time together. He will remain very special to me, and I am sorry for always nagging him to turn the football over. I didn't mind it so much really.

All kinds of people will come into your life. Some will hurt you and make you feel like you're constantly on a terrifying Alton Towers ride. Some will fix the broken pieces of your soul back together and be your pillar of strength. And some will look so much like a Disney prince that you will want to keep them in a little box forever. (But you can't – I should really stress that.)

In the end, I realised that in relationships – be they long and intense or short and exciting – will shape you. With each one I evolved into a different version of myself, and for each one I learned a little bit more about who I am. I think the one that will last is when you've learned enough about yourself to not settle. I will always have a lot of love in my heart and will fall quickly, I just do and I will always let something go that isn't meant for me, eventually. Even if that is really fucking hard.

How to Get
Over Someone

Days 1–4:

Stock your house with your favourite foods and plenty of wine. It's definitely acceptable to buy all this either in your pyjamas or in clothes he/she left behind at yours. If you can't move, voice-note a shopping list to your best friend. If your best friend isn't around, download Deliveroo.

Your sofa can become your new best friend for a few days. Take a load off. Netflix was invented for days like these (it wasn't but I like to think it might have been). Whatever you do, DO NOT watch *The Notebook*. DO NOT WATCH THE NOTEBOOK. Watch *Making A Murderer*.

'Anyone around?' If you are at home, alone, newly heartbroken and wanting some company – send that message. If you are at home, with your boyfriend/girlfriend on the sofa and you receive that message, that is the message from a newly single friend who needs to go out. You better wash your bum and get the Rimmel instant on because you're going out in support of the heartbroken. Sorry love.

For the heartbroken ones – go easy on your friends. Even if as soon as you rock up to the pub someone says 'So how's Adam?' – when they've forgotten Adam is a fuckwit who has been sending dick pics to a girl he met in Ibiza. Yes, I know your heart is now crushed like a Rice Krispie cake you've dropped on the floor and then ground into the carpet, but your friends will need some time to adjust and not everybody has the words.

Days 5–9:

Wash your hair, tidy your room, if you're feeling up to it change your bed sheets. Message your friends, 'I'm making pasta,' and have them all round to chat. I do suggest cooking, it's therapeutic and distracting and I think you'll enjoy it. Something simple though, this isn't the time to try and master a soufflé. 'The thing is I kind of always knew it wasn't right,' someone will say. 'Honestly, be glad this has happened now and not in six months,' will say another.

Limit yourself to only an hour of stalking his social media a day. Don't go cold turkey, but don't overdose either. In fact, no delete him. (I'm not great at this am I!)

When your friends have gone, have a bath, listen to a podcast, light a scented candle. Shave your legs, paint your nails – giving yourself that bit of care and attention will make you feel loved. Self care, sister.

Days 10–14:

Go on, head out into the night, but delete his/her number first. Let's be honest, before you delete it you're going to write down the number on a bit of paper and put it in your knicker drawer. You will still be able to find your knicker drawer at three in the morning after a BNO. And nowadays deleting some-one's number is not deleting someone's number – you will find it, in an archive somewhere. But at least try to!

Eat your tea before you go out. White wine-no tea is a disaster. Try not to sleep with someone because your heart will still be sore. But if you do sleep with someone, remember, protection is your friend. Getting pregnant or an STI at this point will not be helpful to your recovery and will guarantee a huge bout of 'hangxiety' the next day.

Days 15–30:

Go to the gym. Cut your hair. Buy yourself new knickers. Work on being healthy and happy and finding out 'what it is you really want'.

Days 31–60:

Have a ponder over dating apps and possibly download some, but also probably delete them as quickly as you swipe right to the fit boy two miles away. A year from now, repeat all the above.

Running the
Rat Race

Christmas is one of my favourite times of the year. As you've probably got the picture by now, my family bloody love a party, and Christmas is an excuse to have a glorious one, and then another one, and then another one, all the way up to New Year. Plenty of booze, plenty of food, plenty of singalongs, a gigantic tree, endless excuses to get tarted up – and plenty of time to recover each day on the sofa in front of *Home Alone* with a medicinal cheese board.

Christmas is also a time when, despite the total joy at the prospect of having Baileys on my Coco-Pops for two weeks, I have often felt reflective and down if I don't have a Christmas-jumper wearing boyfriend by my side to shower with presents and to sleep on a blow-up bed with.

It's so annoying. I've got my health, my family, my friends, my cheeseboard … What more could I possibly need!?

Then, the old Christmas engagements start popping up. I'm here in a Santa hat and Mum telling me off for coming in late and eating all the ham whilst girls two, three years younger than me are putting up ring selfies in the park with 'A perfect

Christmas' as the caption. Oh hell. (Sidenote: I've always wanted a Christmas wedding, I want the snow, the sparkling decorations, the trees, *Home Alone* music playing as I walk down the aisle …)

Christmas can be hard when you are without a significant other. I just wish we could all be happy at the *exact same time*. When we were growing up, everything happened to everyone at a similar point. Sure, some people got periods when they were nine and some people got them when they were 15, but no one's really racing for the time when wearing white knickers becomes a case of Russian roulette. When we're younger, we all grow a little taller each year, we all finish school and move on to new things at the same time, we're all on the same trajectory together. But unfortunately, that doesn't happen when it comes to relationships. Gutted.

Parking the tragedy of the situation for now, logistically it's a pain in the arse, isn't it? Why were we not taught at school that from our mid-twenties onwards we should have taken out an ISA and started saving just for all the weddings we'll need to cover? Alternatively, the lesson could have been: limit your friends to five – five is a number you can just about cover. If you have more than five friends, I'm afraid you can kiss goodbye to being able to afford a deposit on a house before you're 35. Especially. Takes deep breath. If you're invited to the hen do . . . This is what will happen:

You are walking down the street one day, minding your own business. Suddenly your phone is burning a hole in your pocket – it's vibrating like there's no tomorrow to the point where you're actually quite enjoying it. But you can't leave it in your pocket, there's clearly some sort of emergency. You pull your phone out and see that, no, the flat you live in is not on fire. Instead you've been invited to a new WhatsApp group by a number you don't recognise. The group is invariably called 'Berlin Bitches'. 'Madrid Mamas'. Or my personal favourite: 'Amsterdaaaaaaam, girl'.

You open up WhatsApp. You were invited to the group at 2.15pm. It is now 2.17pm and you already have SEVEN HUNDRED messages. The group admin – the maid of honour – is nearly always a girl called Bex, and she is the dictionary definition of passive aggressive. On the surface, she's the loveliest person you've ever met, but underneath every word she's bubbling with rage. She's like a Rottweiler with a St Tropez spray tan that's getting darker by the hour. What Bex wants more than anything is for you to part with exactly £1,378 asap – and, no, don't you dare suggest waiting for payday, anyone who does categorically hates the bride. You may indeed ask what the £1,378 is going to get you: you'll be flying to a capital city or beach resort somewhere in Europe and staying in an Airbnb with no windows and one too few bunk beds. Yes, it does include something else: the bride's portion of the bill – she deserves it because she's found the love of her life and is incredibly happy, whereas everyone else is a failure and must pay their own way. Except everyone who has already got married – you're just being generous.

The itinerary, which you can have an opinion about so long as you keep it to yourself, will be something along the lines of a boozy boat trip with the first watered-down gin and tonic free, a pole-dancing class where Bex and anyone else who goes to the gym can show off their skills, a jaunt to a male strip show with a very beige buffet and plenty of games such as penis piñata, which, yes, you will also be expected to contribute money to. The cost of all this plus food and alcohol will likely be another £932. AND, YES, YOU WILL BE PAYING FOR THE BRIDE.

Over £2,000 and three days of your life spent with people you'd never choose to hang around with and you'll never get back later, you can start looking forward to the actual wedding day. After you've sorted the gift, outfit, travel and hotel, you don't know when you'll be able to go on a holiday you'd actually like to go on, with people you'd choose to go with, ever again. But, of course, the actual wedding is beautiful. The bride looks stunning, there's an open bar (warning: not all weddings come with these) and the speeches have all been amazing. You felt a little tremble in your gut looking around at the other smug couples gazing wistfully at each other while the bride and her new husband said their vows, but you're really riding the wave of love.

Now you're looking around your table of fellow singletons. Your mum likely said something to you along the lines of, 'Ooo, you're going to a wedding? Might meet a nice man!' Ha, as if life is that kind! There are only two specimens on your table to choose from: the rogue cousin from America they don't like but couldn't *not* invite, and a guy you slept with five years ago who struggled to keep it up with a condom on. If push comes to shove, all right, you'll take that one for the team, but now you've paid the expense of a double room it might be better just to make the most of having it all to yourself. Or not.

The entirety of this experience is then repeated as many as four times in a summer. If you do eventually get a boyfriend, you will have to add another four to your calendar for his friends, meaning all your weekends in June and July will no longer belong to you.

An unmarried friend of mine recently reminded me that 50 per cent of marriages end in divorce these days. She seemed to find solace in this, whereas all it made me think was, 'Oh my God, by the time I'm 35, half my friends will get divorced and then remarry and I'll have to do this routine ALL OVER AGAIN.'

Deep down I *know* getting married doesn't equal any sort of success, but then why does life seem like a race towards it? I *know* that when a friend of mine gets married it doesn't take away the likelihood of me doing the same, but it does feel like a big flashing sign reminding me I haven't done it yet. Who sets these rules? Who makes us feel this way? Why does someone being happy, even when we love them to absolute bits, make us feel a little bit sad?

I don't have the answers. What I hope is that soon the adult train we're on will magically take me through a station where I'll learn not to compare the milestones I've completed with other people's.

But.

If I'm really, *really* honest.

I think I'd rather just marry a beautiful man and be too busy being blinded by my fuck-off engagement ring to look out of the window when we get there.

Under Pressure

Being in the entertainment industry is like running continuously on an uphill treadmill, the gradient gets higher and higher and your feet move faster and faster. You get one job that you're really happy about, but no one really wants to talk about it – they just want to know what you're doing next. There's no sitting still, ever. It's like constantly battling for a promotion but, instead of it being every year, it's every month. Each job has to be more splashy, more sparkly, more noisy than the last, and if you don't keep the fireworks popping then you run the danger of being forgotten about and becoming irrelevant. Like a Catherine wheel. Like a Catherine wheel that's whirling and fizzing around but not really going anywhere. No big bang. No big ooo-aaaa moment. A bit like a sparkler, you have a small window to wave it around while the light burns bright, but do it quick, because in a few moments time, you'll be withered and burnt out and chucked in a bucket to cool off.

OK, maybe I'm being a bit dramatic, but that's kind of my job.

All this pressure does have an effect on you, it can't not. It does for everyone. It also means you're constantly left feeling a bit unsatisfied. I was quite lucky, to be honest, with how my career kicked off because most actors have to graft for a long time before they get a big break, but my big break came when I first started out. And, after *The Inbetweeners* and *Dancing on Ice*, opportunities did start rolling in, but I think everyone was waiting for me to get this huge movie. I kept getting parts and being told, 'This'll be the big one. This'll be the big one.' I am so proud of all the films I've been in and I loved doing them, but none of them were blockbusters. And it got so exhausting waiting for the biggun to come. In the end it's what led me to making different choices – going on *I'm a Celeb* ... and deciding to give my own one-woman show a go.

I could have tried harder, that's something I will always have to accept – and I have. I could have trained; I could have read Shakespeare; I could have gone to more plays and studied them; I could have eaten less. But I was never going to be *that* person. I'm sure I've only ever got to where I am through being 100 per cent entirely Emily Atack. I worked with my assets. I was blonde, I had boobs, I was slim: there will always be roles for those girls. There will always be *FHM* covers for those girls. It worked for me and I've never regretted doing it. I look

188

back now as a woman and roll my eyes and think, 'It shouldn't be that way', but it was – and I'm not complaining at all. I've got the *FHM* plaques up in my house and I'm proud of them. I truly believe that everything I've done – taking my top off, being a bit of a pin-up for a while – has led me to where I am now. And where I am now is sitting on my squidgy arse on a sofa, looking back at those photos going, 'Phwoar, I looked good – let's all have a good laugh that I used to pose in my pants like that.' It's all material now for my stand-up!

I got enough jobs to keep me ticking over, and through doing that and not bullying myself into starving my body for the perfect role, I think I actually maintained the elusive work-life balance. I was never going to choose not to go to my friend's birthday and drink vat-loads of wine with her before an audition – I knew there would be girls going for the same part as me who were as good as me or better and that there was a chance I'd get it, and a chance I wouldn't. I wasn't going to put all my eggs in the work basket and not see the smile on my friend's face when I bought the 17th round of tequilas. Life was too short then and it's too short now. If I didn't get it, I didn't get it – there were other gigs. And to be honest, without wanting to sound big-headed, I don't think I ever lost out on an audition because I was hanging out of my arse. I've never had bad feedback from an audition. If I didn't get a part, I think it was because I didn't fit sometimes: my weight, my background. There's a lot of rejection in acting, and it can hurt if you really want the part and you've demonstrated your commitment by not going to the pub with your mates the night before. But it makes you stronger; you pick yourself up and get on with it, you count your lucky stars that there have been roles before, you trust there will be roles again. It gives you more and more armour until you're brave enough to make leaps you might not have taken otherwise.

In 2014, there were a few scary months where I was getting rejected for everything. Good, but not good enough. I was reaching the end of my tether with it all. The audition for *Dad's Army* was approaching, and then something awful happened: a really wonderful, dear friend of mine died in a car crash. I was devastated. He was only 30. I spent the weekend afterwards with all my friends, hugging one another, sobbing, utterly heartbroken. The audition was on a Monday and there was no way I could go. I looked at myself in the mirror, puffy-eyed and grey, feeling so lost and empty, and thought, 'There is no way I can do this.'

It's such a cliché for people to say that a person who's died would have wanted them to carry on, not to put off doing something, but no jokes I felt like I could hear him saying, in his Essex accent, 'Don't be such a silly fucker. Go to the audition.'

For the first time, I knew I really didn't care if I didn't get the part. Rejection just didn't matter compared to this tragedy that had cleaved my heart in two. So I decided to go. I marched into that room, I had no nerves whatsoever, and I probably gave the best audition I've ever given. I got the part.

People like to quote sayings such as 'If at first you don't succeed, try, try and try again' and 'Nothing worth having comes easy'. It's taken me years to realise it, but I don't believe in any of that. Do your best – do *your* best. If it works out, it was meant to be; if it doesn't, try again, but if you can't be bothered to try again, don't worry about it. Maybe decide on a different path. There are plenty to choose from. There's so much pressure nowadays to kill ourselves at work, or to achieve a goal we're actually not as bothered about as we think we are. If this resonates with you, don't let it get to you. Some industries, like acting, are uphill treadmills. If you don't want to run on them, don't be afraid to get off.

The People
Who Shaped Me:
Grandma Doris

Doris is my dad's mum and she's my last living grandparent. She lives in Yorkshire and has done her whole life, and for many years ran a clothes shop in her local town centre. A stunning woman with bags of style – her wardrobe is to die for. At 87, Grandma Doris still puts on her make-up and diamond earrings and goes on cruises and long holidays to exotic locations. She still spends hours on the phone, chatting to friends each night. She's the sort of lady who you'll find nattering away to a shopkeeper and, when you ask her how they know each other as you leave, she'll reply, 'Oh I don't know him, love.'

She is the stereotypical proud grandparent in every sense of the word – our school photos line the walls and surfaces of her immaculate bungalow and she still sends birthday cheques to us in the post even though by our age all her kids were parents themselves. In a big silver frame on the table in her hallway, next to the house phone, is a blown-up photo of me, my dad ... and John Barrowman at the *I'm a Celeb* ... wrap party! (Impressed by the quick printing technique there, Doris.)

For my cousin Faith's hen do, Grandma Doris and her friend joined her and 15 girls in Las Vegas. She marched up and down that strip and stayed up late on the slots – she doesn't even drink so that is some epic stamina. One night, at the strip show the girls had organised, one of the giant muscly men yanked her onto the stage and performed the Magic Mike 'Pony' dance on her lap. I think she kissed him on the lips!

She lives on her own now, but cared for my grandad Roy for years at their house before he went into a care home. Grandma Doris and Grandad Roy married young and raised my dad Keith, his identical twin Tim and their brother Simon well, surrounded by music – all three are exceptionally talented musicians and can play just about every instrument there is. I only ever knew my grandad Roy as an older man; he suffered two very big strokes when I was young and so I was only ever really aware of him being slightly held back by ailments. But he was a funny and talented man who I loved very much.

I've taken a lot from my grandma Doris – or I try very hard to. She's a bright, strong, ballsy and beautiful woman who doesn't let life knock her. I am so lucky to have her – she, out of everyone in the family, is my biggest fan. She follows it all, she watches every show I do and I'm pretty sure that, through her systematic canvassing at her local market, she was personally responsible for 50 per cent of the votes I received in the final of *I'm a Celeb* ....

'I'm Depressed'

The Depressed

These are two words I hear a lot, and I'm sure you do too. I use them all the time and my friends do too. Correct me if I'm wrong, but 'I'm depressed' OFTEN means in young people's terms 'I'm hungover' or 'I wish I hadn't done that' or 'I've got so much work to do and I haven't done it cos I've been getting pissed all weekend'. But sometimes it may just mean something more than that.

From a very young age I've felt susceptible to sadness, feeling scared, anxious, like I want to cry all the time, and I didn't know why. I've always been a happy person in general. Anyone who knows me will usually describe my personality as 'bubbly' and 'outgoing' and 'fun', and, sorry to sound like David Brent here, but, yes, I am all of those things, sure. However, there's always been something inside me somewhere that feels like a lost kid in a supermarket. You know, that sinking feeling you get the first time you lose your mum in a supermarket and you think your world is about to end and you can't get past the never-ending sense of doom and emptiness. I sometimes feel like that – I feel lost, I feel homesick for a home that doesn't exist, I feel like I want to go home but I don't know where that is, even though I have a million homes surrounding me full of people I love and that I could go back to whenever I please. I still feel like something is missing and that there's an empty hole somewhere in me, and I've pretty much always felt that way.

I remember listening to music and it really affecting me, as did films and the stories my mum would read to me or make up on the spot. I was sensitive and very open to feelings, which has been a great thing in my life and makes me empathetic, but it has also at times been to my detriment. I find myself, and always have, getting very emotionally invested in things. When it comes to happiness, I fully commit to that emotion when I'm feeling upbeat, but the same thing happens when I'm feeling sad, and I fully commit to that too.

I've found that the majority of people in the creative industry are this way; my parents and most members of my family have been like this. As I've grown up and become more knowledgeable about the word 'depressed', and learnt about chemical imbalances in the brain, or traumatic pasts and various other causes of depression, I've always tried to ask myself what the reasons are for my feelings. I've felt like this at times since I can remember even having thoughts. I remember once we were putting up our Christmas stockings for Santa when I was about six or seven, and I recall feeling so happy that I actually felt sad. I was heartbreakingly happy. I was crushed with love for my mum as I watched her put the carrots and brandy out on the side for Santa; my heart broke for my dad as I watched him (terribly) putting up the last of the lights in a bush outside our house. And the amount of presents we got!! I've always been funny with presents. I don't have a materialistic bone in my body so I never really fully appreciate a present. Does that make any sense? I feel like someone else should have my present, someone who needs it. I don't need a present. Christmas morning, devastated. So fucking happy and yet devastated at the same time – WHY?! I'm crying as I even write this. It's bizarre. I guess with me, when something makes me happy, I am so terrified of it being taken from me. Nothing in terms of material possessions (I honestly couldn't give a shit if my house got burgled tomorrow – I would hope that someone who was desperate enough to nick my stuff now has a couch to sit on; I can get another one) – it's my family, my mum and dad, my siblings, my past, my future even. The fear of having any of those things taken from me fills me with dread every day. Subconsciously, mainly – I'm not saying I sit there sobbing all day, every day, about all these things.

I think this is what confuses people about 'depression', its insidious nature. Some of the greatest comedians in the world have been the most depressed, it doesn't discriminate – funny people, or the richest or most famous, or someone who seems on the surface to have everything they could wish for, anyone can suffer from it. 'What have you got to be depressed about?' is a question I hear a lot – and it really pisses me off. It's absolutely nothing to do with what you do or don't have in your life. It's like someone saying, 'What have you got a migraine for? There's no reason to have one.' You can't explain it, you just have a migraine.

I think, for me, I never want to tell anyone I sometimes suffer from feeling like this because I'm known as being so happy, and I don't want to disappoint anyone, or I don't want them to think my whole outward persona is false. It really isn't. When I'm at a party or a barbie, or at work, or in a jungle, I really am presenting to you my true self, which is a friendly and happy person. I identify myself as a happy individual who loves life and loves People, Places and Things (that play's a bit depressing, though!).

I just sometimes feel sad and I can't really explain why. I've had therapy, I've been on antidepressants, stopped boozing for periods of time, been to the gym every single January, read self-help books ... and I've come to realise that actually just accepting that sometimes I feel this way is way less stressful than always trying to figure it out. 'It's okay not to be okay' and all that.

I think we're all now made to think we should be running around with unicorns up our arses when, actually, sometimes maybe we just have to accept that we might feel shit sometimes, and at specific periods more than others. Some days it's just a little bit more difficult to get out of bed, and I'm just learning to be at peace with that. You can do things to help yourself along the way, like put olives in a bowl, light a candle and put a facemask on, or listen to your favourite Spice Girls song.

Being fearful of my past and my future will probably always creep in every now and then, but I'm learning to embrace the *now*, whether I am in a good or bad place mentally. Because I'm here, I am alive. Because now is MY present, and the now is the greatest gift of all.

Sister, Sister

So you've heard a lot about Martha. The sister, the agent, the fun police. So here she is in her own words. Marf (as we call her) might be scary boss lady now but just to really embarrass her, I'm pleased to say that her nickname as a baby was psycho sausage because she looked like an uncooked sausage. She was a large baby, had no teeth for ages, and was always cackling like a mad old man. If you are lucky enough to have a sister you are close to you will know that it's impossible to describe the relationship and do it justice in words. Impossible. No other person can make you flip your lid like it but you'd drop everything to be there for them, Over to you, Marf.

I was meant to start writing this chapter last night but I had to postpone it until this morning as I was up until just gone midnight scrolling through over 18,000 images on an old iCloud account of Emily's.

A few weeks ago, one spring Saturday morning while I was drying my hair with Saturday Kitchen on in the background (it was a non-hangover, smug kind of Saturday), Emily called me. If Emily calls me before are we there yet?

11am on a Saturday (or most days, in fact) I know that a) something is probably very wrong or b) she hasn't been to bed yet. I answered and she said with panic and a break in her voice, 'There's naked pictures of me on Twitter.' My stomach lurched, I am silent. I looked, yep, there they were. A few RTs, a few faves, many, many absolutely vile comments.

We soon establish these are from iCloud, an old one, hacked and leaked online. Fuck.

I would expect most people would have their sister as their first port of call should their breasts somehow have made their way onto the internet against their will, so nothing unusual there. But the difference here is that it's not only my personal duty to help her with this issue, but my professional one too.

I am one of Emily's agents/managers. Her little sister first and foremost – but, along with a guy named Alex Segal, I manage and represent Emily in her working life. We would call ourselves 'her people' if we were dicks.

Much like a real leak from your bathroom, the next few hours were spent going down the usual pathways to try to assess the root of the problem and contain the damage caused by the leak. We summon a conference call with her publicists to discuss the matter. One by one people get added on the line: 'Hi James', 'Hi

Marth' – everyone sounds like they've been out last night, much less bright-eyed and bushy-tailed than if this was a Monday call. We talk numbers – how many pics? Two? Three? Eighty-seven? 'Emily, do you think there's anything worse on there?' We call a lawyer; he joins in the conference call: 'Hi Jonathan.' We pay through the nose for said lawyer. We get a call from the Sun. We call Apple. We call Mum (awkward).

So, for now, Smug-Saturday is on hold. I had planned to get coffee and browse around H&M with my fiancé Mark, but that will have to wait until tomorrow. He gets it. Between myself, Alex, Emily's publicists, her lawyer, we make a plan and assign roles – you check this, I'll look at that, I'll call her back. I am never anything but astounded by the speed and the efficiency of the people I work with. There is not a single weak link in the chain in Team Emily.

Where were we? Oh yes, the violation of Emily's sexual privacy. The reason I am recalling this story is because in this business of show it is so easy to forget the crux of what you are dealing with. The job is to put out the fire – you often forget the fuel at the pit of the blaze. Emily, her private photos, her body, put out to the public against her will. It's just awful. Emily has to recount stories to men she barely knows about what parts of her body might appear on Twitter next. She has to (in detail) let us know of anything she feels may come to light. It's embarrassing and it's humiliating.

As her manager, her agent, during these operational moments to put out the fire I forget that she's my sister, and I think it's important I have that separation – otherwise our working relationship wouldn't work. But once the team have gone back to their Saturday trip to the zoo and back to their newspapers and tea (until tomorrow's papers land), I am always left with a feeling of such horror for my sister – not my client – but my big sister. I want to wrap her up in cotton wool. I ask if she's okay. She always says yes.

So, last night, at midnight after we got access to the hacked files, I sat and I went through each photo one by one. Selfie, selfie, selfie, pics of our baby sister, more pics of baby sister, Mum, Dad, selfie, selfie, selfie, night out, night out, night out, hangover photo, hangover photo. This is not just her life, but our life, our life as a family, and for someone to have access to those private moments, 95 per cent of which have not been shared on Instagram – so were never intended to be in the public domain – made me feel sad. Pics of our brother in hospital strapped to a machine, pics of our late uncle Simon, pics of our grandad, pics of our uncle Steve on his last day of radiotherapy, pics of moments we have shared not with her followers or fans for likes or for RTs but private moments snapped and shared on WhatsApp or kept sacred in a folder marked 'Family <3'. Someone has all of these, someone somewhere has them all. When someone in the public eye gets their privacy violated it has a ripple effect throughout that person's whole world.

Working with family has taught me to be a good manager, I care for everyone I look after with a great deal of intimacy and empathy as if they were family. I care for every person as if they were Emily as best as I can. She sets the benchmark.

Working together has always been part of the plan. Even as toddlers I'd push her around in a pram even though I was 18 months younger. I would stage-manage Emily as a kid in the garden and ensure her performance in the paddling pool was perfected before she went on and entertained a good turnout of kids from the village. I never wanted to be famous or in the public eye but Emily did. She couldn't really do anything else but perform.

I am particularly proud of her achievements that perhaps didn't gain her the huge profile she has now. Away from the jungle, away from the hype, the fake tan and celebrity men, she has quality jewels in her comedy crown that I'll always be envious of. She has worked closely with comedy legends, including Victoria Wood, Julia Davis, Tracey Ullman, Ben Elton, Bill Nighy, Toby Jones and Jennifer Saunders. Many of these people hired her personally after rounds of auditions. She has captured casting directors' eyes and won roles by her quick and effortless comedy timing and the sparkle in her eye. When she was cast as Daphne in the remake of Dad's Army among the lead cast (alongside Catherine Zeta-bloody-Jones), I nearly exploded. She looked sensational in that blonde wig and army gear, like she was plucked from that era. We saw pap shots of her online, marching along this huge set-up final shot alongside Michael Gambon, Sarah Lancashire and Felicity Montagu (as a huge Alan Partridge fan the fact she was working with Lynn was almost too much for me). In the end titles, on her freeze-frame 'You have been watching ... Emily Atack' I burst into tears at the screening.

These are the moments where I am her sister, not her agent. I often have to keep a poker face when she achieves great things – nobody wants a manager who actually secretly wants to be the talent, even worse if you're their sister, cringe. So, I keep calm and collected, but of course I scream and jump around and tell my fiancé about all her achievements when I get home each night.

When she came runner-up to the great Harry Redknapp in I'm a Celeb ..., I was in a tent in Australia with my dad, gripping his arm, while Mum was up on the bridge waiting to greet her. We were down at the base of the camp, watching on a screen with all of the families. When they announced John Barrowman had come third I was stunned. Runner-up – oh my God, Emily, you've done it. Watching her wild knotted hair and freckly, tear-stained, skinny face – that new face everyone was talking about was one I knew so, so well – come second was one of the proudest moments of my life. I am her sister in those instants, not her agent.

Being so close in age meant we shared almost everything growing up, friends, a bedroom, clothes. Everything except our taste in boys. Even at the age of 11 I couldn't fathom Emily wanting to hang around in the back of someone's Vauxhall Nova in a sea of McDonald's wrappers and smoke. The only time Emily hasn't wanted me around was from the age of about ten to 13. She was very naughty in these days and hung around with boys with crispy curtains and gold teeth and push bikes, and they all smoked. I didn't dislike these boys, in fact some were quite entertaining, and I think some of them thought I was quite funny, but I always felt like it was time to go home after an hour of chatting at a gate at the park. I wanted to go back to Mum and dance on the kitchen table (which we often did when nobody was at home).

I was fascinated by Emily's looks as a kid. She looked far too old for her age. But it was enchanting; in middle school she looked like a pop star. I used to steal her clothes a lot, much to Emily's dislike, and, in all honesty, they didn't really fit. I had a bit of a belly and buck teeth and Emily had a washboard stomach and a padded bra and white eyeliner.

I remember once wearing a light-pink halterneck top of hers to the park à la Mariah Carey in the 'Heartbreaker' video. Upon my arrival on my micro scooter, my can of cream soda in hand, an older naughty boy with a Slipknot hoodie shouted 'Belly's gunna get ya!' at me. I didn't really understand what he meant, but soon clocked that he was talking about my pink puppy roll that was proudly sticking out from beneath the top. Emily was greeted with wolf whistles and playful nudges.

I once saw her kissing a boy by the village hall – it stopped me in my tracks. I had never seen her kiss anyone before, I was traumatised. I remember thinking I wasn't sure Father Christmas would like that.

I remember climbing into a tent around the back of a load of garages where Emily was hanging out one summer day; she told me to go away. I declined to listen and stuffed myself into the hot green cocoon. Boys without tops on – I remember thinking their nipples were very dark in comparison to our brother George's who (at the time) was like a little pink micro pig. Within five minutes of me taking up too much room a boy who looked a bit like a lizard, was making wisecracks and laughing at me under his breath; he then kindly pointed out that I had very hairy legs. I looked down at my milk bottle bruised legs stretched out in front of me, covered in a moss of white wisps – he was right and I was embarrassed; it was time to leave. I went home immediately and hacked my legs to bits with Dad's Bic razor and got very told off by Mum when she found hairs and blood in the bath. In a bid to completely turn the bollocking around I explained to Mum that Emily was hanging around with scary lizard boys and kissing them in the tents down by the garages. Needless to say, Kate dragged her home and Emily banned me from hanging out with them for the rest of the summer holidays.

Their loss. While I used grassing up Emily as a good bid to take the heat off me for my impromptu summer shave, I remember telling mum because really I wanted Emily to come home. I didn't like that tent, or those boys. It wasn't right. It would be best if she came home and played with me and George for the rest of the evening in the garden and had some Cheerios.

Moments like that as a younger sister shape you. As a younger sister you watch on, you see how your sister, the person you are most like in the whole world, moves so differently, is received differently. In a weird way I began to realise that if I was uncomfortable, it couldn't be good for Emily. For example, in the tent, I was sure they weren't nice lads, I knew it wasn't fun, but Emily was so relaxed and consumed by the situation that she couldn't see the boys from the lizards! I had a genuine fear I may never see her again. Lost forever in the tents.

It was like I was beginning to lay little concrete blocks within me. If I didn't like it, it can't be good for her. So on I went, for the next 20 years, and I still do to this very day. Laying the blocks and building up the fortress that I use time and time again to shield her from the shit when bad things come to a head.

Tom, Jason, Daniel, bullies, school, admin, home-work, morning-after pills, and now work, you name it – I am there with operation 'Help Emily' whenever she needs it. As teens I learnt to drive, I printed her scripts, I cut up pillow cases to make headscarves for her auditions when we realised at the last minute the casting notes said '1950s'. The one time I had nothing to give her and the fortress closed for the season was during our parents' divorce. Emily put a roof over our head, she made the phone calls, she brought the Domino's pizza, she paid the council tax (sometimes) and she held it together while I fell apart. She saved me.

And so, here we are today, and really nothing has changed – I'm still trying to get her out of tents with guys. I am still in awe of her when she walks onto a red carpet. I feel I have a lifetime of experience to make the right call for her, but sometimes I get it wrong, sometimes I need to let it go. It pains me to tell you but I was on the fence about the jungle; she was certain that it was the year to do it and she was right.

I'm getting married next year and Emily will of course be my maid of honour and by my side on the day. I sometimes think she is worried she's losing me, but, married or not, the fortress will always be open.

It's a Jungle
Out There

Taking part in *I'm A Celebrity* ... is one of the most insane things I've ever done. You do often forget that it is a TV show – the biggest one on UK television, in fact. So while you see the bugs and the hammocks and cold showers you are also part of a major operation. It's thrilling, it's HUGE. Here's a few bits you may not know about The Jungle experience.

- I slept the best I have ever slept in my life in that camp. While this might not be the juicy gossip you were after, I thought that was extremely telling about how we live our lives normally. The second my head hit the pillow I was out. For eight, nine sometimes ten hours. The fresh air, the exercise, the warmth no doubt helps, but I felt such peace of mind. No phone making your eyes ache, no Twitter making you feel anxious, no emails, no digital invasion, no alcohol, no sugar. My mind would drift into peaceful, light dreams (usually of food). You have an alarm clock in there (yes even in the Jungle someone is getting you out of bed). 'WAKEY WAKEY CAMPERS RISE AND

SHINE,' the voice of Gods would boom out across these huge tannoys every morning. Well I guess it's fair enough, they did have a show to make every day.

- 'EMILY, GET UP!' the voice would boom after 40 minutes of me not stirring. Everyone else would be slowly getting up, bleary eyed, walking to the shower. Not me, I'd roll back over, back into this soft, pure slumber that I cherished. I haven't slept that well since and I probably never will, but I learned what true peaceful sleep is in there, and it means pretty much getting rid of everything in our life that we consume too much of.

- The hunger is real. You only eat what you win, and other than that, it's beans and rice. We all got on brilliantly but food can cause even the smiliest of campmates to kick off and get narky. After making it to the final with Harry and John you get to order your dream meal – it is cooked from scratch by a chef and you can order whatever you fancy. My meal – starter: Baked Camembert with sweet onion chutney and bread (and half of John Barrowman's pizza). Main: an American style stacked burger with bacon, cheese, onions, relish and sweet potato fries. Dessert: I was craving peanut butter and chocolate and cream so I had them whip up a a chocolate and peanut butter cheesecake! I then had some of Harry's sticky toffee pudding too. For my drink I had a glass of cold Provence rosé (my fave wine). It went straight to my head, I was giddy, I was in heaven. I think it was one of the best moments of my life. No, in fact, Harry gave me his Bailey's – and then THAT was the best moment of my life.

– The money is great, but for me I was probably one of the lowest paid of the series. When you have legends like Noel Edmonds, Harry Redknapp, Nick Knowles in there you can kind of gather that you're probably in the bargain basement! But I hope they think they got good bang for their buck! Haha.

– The security guards are fit. Whenever you do a task you have security with you and some of them were HUNKS. Like action man hunks. After three weeks of no action, your eyes start wandering! I got told off for trying to chat to one of the guys when I was being taken down to a task – trust me to seriously attempt to go on the pull in the jungle, smelling like pond water with dreadlocks. They aren't allowed to speak back to you, nobody is, not the crew, not the camera guys – definitely not the fit security guards. I saw one of them at the wrap party, one I had seen a few times while in there. After a lot of champagne I made a beeline to go and chat to him but within 30 seconds my dad appeared and dragged me away! Killjoy.

– Lock down was wonderful, contrary to popular belief. You have a few days before you go in – you hand over your phone, your luggage and then you just wait. I was in a hotel for a few days alone with nothing to do but read and wait. Wait for someone to come and collect me and tell me 'it's time'. I was excited. But let me tell you I absolutely hated jumping out of that plane. It hurt, I was absolutely terrified, the harness crushed my vagina and I'm still picking the wedgy out of my arse.

Love

Being *in* love – what does it mean?

Since I was about four years old, I've been aware of love in my heart. When I was about six I started to dance with my curtains in my bedroom, and wrap them around me pretending they were my boyfriend/Aladdin. I would have dreams of being loved by a Disney prince, and wake up completely devastated that it was just a dream. I would weep for hours at a time over the boy band Hanson (the long-haired kids that looked like actual pretty females) and then, a bit later on, any Westlife song would send me over the edge. I cried constantly over boys at school, I'd develop crushes on waiters on family holidays; I constantly felt like I was lovesick.

As a grown woman, I'm not that different. I might not dance with my curtains anymore (only on Fridays ...), but I constantly find myself in a state of despair about being 'in love'. I'm now approaching 30, trying to figure out what that really means. Here's what I have so far.

When you are *in* love, you are *in* something. Then I thought, 'What else can you say you are *in* other than love?' When I googled 'I am in ...', searching for alternatives, this is what I found:

- I am in ... search of
- I am in ... need of
- I am in ... debt
- I am in ... trouble

It almost seems like when you are *in* something, you are lost and out of control of the situation – meaning when you are in, you can't get out. So maybe when we casually declare, 'I am in love', we should really think about what we are saying.

I've definitely been in love before, and every time I have, I've been lost in it, no control. I'm searching for it, I need it, I am lost without it. I am in debt to it. Then I thought, 'I *have* so much! I *have* so much! What if I *had* love instead? Maybe *having* love is something that can bring happiness?'

If you say you have something, it implies that it is already yours, you are in possession of it. If you met someone and said, 'Yeah, he's great, we have love', surely that would be better than being *in* love because it's something you both confidently share?

Falling in love – that phrase has already set itself up for a negative. Falling – when you fall, you hurt

230

yourself, or at least you nearly hurt yourself. Falling can NEVER be a good outcome, and yet I constantly just stick plasters on the wounds and chuck myself onto the spiky rocks, hoping that one day someone will catch me, or I will at least land safely.

I don't think we can have aims in love because there are all different types. I think in the past I have definitely confused love with lust. I have lusted after relationships that I cannot fully have, and I became addicted to that hit of euphoria every time I had them for even a small amount of time. And so, because of that intensity, I thought it was love. I thought pain was love, and chaos, and longing, and if I didn't feel those things about someone, I thought, 'Well, I can't be in love then.' It was like I needed the pain and uncertainty to be fulfilled or to keep me interested.

In the Ancient Greek language, there are different words for different types of love, and there are at least four ways to describe the concept of love in its various forms:

Agape – The love religious people have between them and God – considered the highest form of love. It's a selfless love.
Eros – intimate, passionate, romantic love.

Philia – the love you feel for your friends.
Storge – familial love, between parents and kids, or between siblings.

As I was reading up about those meanings, it did make me realise that if you are a very loving person, a very 'deep' person who explores all kinds of chambers and tombs of feelings, you will go through life and feel every single type of love. Some people don't. Maybe some only experience a more 'basic' version of it. Some people's hearts and heads just don't open those scary doors because it might possibly be just too terrifying for them to fathom.

Unfortunately for me (or fortunately, some might say), I have always been a daredevil when it comes to my heart. I play with fire, get burnt, make the same mistakes, move on and make new ones, and I am open to emotion, making me completely susceptible to pain. The phrase 'I wear my heart on my sleeve' doesn't even begin to cover it. I hand my heart over on a royal red fluffy cushion while I'm down on my knees, hoping and praying that it will be enough for someone, and enough for them to know that, although broken, it doesn't give in, it's everlasting.

What I'm slowly learning is that I am, and will ALWAYS be, this way. It's something I cannot change. I have so much love in my heart I literally sometimes don't know where to put it all, so it spills out of me like lava. And, just like lava, people run from it, terrified. But I'm learning to just accept and be okay with that. You can change a lot of things – you can even educate your brain to become more knowledgeable by having therapy and reading self-help books etc. – but your heart isn't one of them. This is the one I have been given – damaged, battered and bruised, but everlasting.

So I will keep loving, tripping, falling, spilling and forever hoping and praying that one day I will find a soft landing.

The People Who Shaped Me: TV-Land Friends

TV friends come and go. You do a job, you fall in love with each other for those few weeks and then you move on. Passing them occasionally on a red carpet or at a party, you give them a quick squeeze and that's about it. Some stick. Leigh Francis, aka Keith Lemon, is one of my dearest pals. Leigh gave me jobs when I really needed them, and saw something in me before anyone else did. He let me be funny, he has never cast me as sexy in any of his shows. He's one of the few blokes who saw through the sexy schoolgirl thing and let me be me. He is an extremely loyal man. As part of his many sketch shows I've been Michelle Keegan to his Mark Wright and Louis Tomlinson to his Harry Styles. We have never pissed ourselves laughing as much as we did when he made me play Slimer in the *Ghostbusters* episode for *The Keith & Paddy Picture Show*. He yelled 'BOGEY GHOST' at me for six hours while I was painted bright green and wearing a bald cap. Leigh is one of the few remaining traditional all-around talents who can do it all; he is hugely successful, clever, artistic and a comedy genius. He's taught me so much over the years and I am so grateful to him.

Other 'TV friends' who I've come to love over the years include Ollie Locke, Holli Dempsey, Jason Maza, Laura Whitmore, Liz Holmwood, Steve Dunne, Joel Dommett, Kieran Richardson, Russel Kane and Daniel Mays – these kinds of familiar faces are the ones you come to rely on. Seeing them pop up at a lonely party makes you instantly know you're on for a good night, and they've thrown me a lot of bones that I won't ever forget.

Alex Johnson, a major film casting director, gave me the role of Daphne in *Dad's Army* and then, two years later, a leading role in a film called *Patrick*, alongside Beattie Edmondson and her mum, Jennifer Saunders. I played a PE teacher in that film who was always eating cream cakes. The director of *Patrick* was called Mandie Fletcher. Mandie stripped me of my make-up – 'Send her back, she looks like a model,' she would say to the make-up team, who would walk me back to the make-up truck to wipe off the tiniest trace of foundation. She would tell me off for 'flirting' in my acting, and spoke to me about how conditioned I was to 'play sexy' – when really she just wanted me to be funny and simply let it all go. 'CUT. GO AGAIN!' she shouted, over and over, take after take. She didn't stop until she had what she wanted. 'Perfect,' she'd then say and wink as I finally found myself. I loved my performance in that movie. No make-up, no love interest, no tits out. I learnt A LOT about myself on that film. It was the last movie I did before *I'm a Celeb* ....

You remember more than anything the moments along the way that make you feel accepted. But then you remember the people and the situations when you felt like a big fake-tanned fish out of water. I feel that girls like me, who wear fake tan, who speak openly about sex, who go out, who watch *Love Island*, who love Ibiza and bottomless brunches, are so often boxed into a corner of stupidity – it's wrong, but you get used to it.

When you're that kind of girl, you're not allowed to be funny, you're not quick, you're not a writer, you're not qualified to speak on social or political issues, you are certainly not a stand-up comedian. I have been booked as the bimbo before and it sucks. After the jungle, I was booked on a late-night chat show and I soon began to feel that I was there to be the butt of the joke – the host seemed frosty, the audience didn't laugh at my jokes, the whole thing felt chaotic. I performed like a circus clown for over two hours, did everything they wanted from me and I just wanted to cry. My agents had told the producers I wouldn't answer any questions about

James Buckley (there had been a story in the press the day before about James and me falling out). Within five minutes of the recording, one of the hosts asked, 'I want to know about James Buckley, what happened there.' The others on the sofa cooed, 'Ooooo.' My face said it all and they moved on quickly and apologised afterwards. They cut it out of the edit but it hurt; it felt like they didn't care about me, or my wishes, or my privacy, it felt like, 'Get the blonde jungle girl on and make her say stupid things.' It made me feel like shit. That is not who I am or who I want to be. I told Martha and Alex. Noted for future.

There is a running theme here about the people who stick around, the good guys and the people you remember along the way, especially in work. You learn to laugh along with the people who can only see the surface-level you – the boobs and the tan – but that's okay. I hope to continue to keep surprising people and showing them there's more to me. I wrote a whole stand-up tour about turning 30, and people actually liked it. The *Guardian* gave me three stars and so did the *Evening Standard* – I would have taken one star for my first show, I'm just happy people came! I write comedy sketches, I do impressions, I sing, act and I love poetry. Look beneath the Estée Lauder Double Wear (best foundation ever) and you might find a smart lady chilling in there – a lady with thoughts, opinions and, dare I say it, the power to do something different.

It seems the people who make an impact on you are the people who really love you for who you are, it's the people who encourage you to be yourself. It's the people who don't just encourage you, but who literally beat your authentic self out of you – like an old dusty rug. At 29, I think finally all of my colours are starting to show through.

What 30
Looked Like ...

At 15

It looked so far away that I didn't give it one speck of thought, except every now and then when a teacher admitted they were 30 and then I thought they were ancient.

At 20

Thirty would be the age when everything was sorted. I'd be living in a mansion with my very rich and beautiful husband and have already pushed out at least one baby and probably be pregnant with another. Martha would be living down the road, also married and with a baby cooking in her tummy, and my double deluxe fridge would be covered in postcards from George. I'd have been in several major movies and my husband would be one of the leads from those films – probably an American who had moved to England because he loved me so much, but luckily we'd held onto his small-massive bolthole on Hollywood Boulevard so we could pop back there routinely.

At 25

Jason and I would be newly married after he proposed to me in Florence. We'd be living in our own flat somewhere in London, thinking about moving out to the country in the near future to live close to his parents. We'd be planning to get pregnant in a year's time if I thought work could take it (I'd be the lead in an ongoing series for ITV by this point, following the success of various British films). Martha would be engaged and living down the road, and my fridge would be too small for the postcards from George so instead they'd be all over the radiator.

At 29

Twenty-nine has been the best year of my life so far. Thirty, I'm sure, will have its own ups and downs, but I feel more in control of everything than I've ever felt before. I don't pretend to know what 30 looks like now. Instead, it is the most breathtakingly beautiful blank page.

10 Reasons
I Know
I'm an Adult

1. I live on my own. I got my own place for the first time recently. It did wonders for my mental health. I did not feel alone, I did not get scared in the night. I cherished my own space and that feeling of total privacy. If you've ever wanted to, and are in the position to, go for it.

2. I save money. Saving is a luxury from a past generation. If you do make sacrifices and save a bit of cash each month, I salute you.

3. I have a new expressed interest in House Plants. It's good for you in that you have to keep them alive . . . and very Instagrammable.

4. I realise that New Year's Eve is 99 per cent of the time the worst night out of the year.

5. I sometimes iron my clothes before I wear them.

6. If I say I'm going home after one or two drinks, I do.

7. I exercise. Much to my dislike I'm learning that this is not optional. Moving your arse means you might live a bit longer. You might feel 10 per cent less sad on a Sunday. I give in to it.

8. I drink more water. Loads of it. Even when I'm not hungover!

9. I accept the things that aren't meant for me – jobs, boys, the last mega loaded nacho at dinner.

10. I'm getting better at remembering birthdays.

10 Reasons
I Know I'm
Not an Adult

1. I'm lying to you about going home after one or two drinks.

2. When something goes wrong, the first thing I want to do is call my mum.

3. I sometimes have to check my Uber receipts after a night out to remember where I came back from.

4. I don't use fabric softener.

5. Phrases like 'switching your Energy tariff', '0% APR' and 'cashback ISA' are a foreign language to me.

6. I still get put on the children's table at Christmas lunch.

7. I can't drive.

8. I still get surprisingly light hangovers.

9. I never pick up my missed parcels from the post office.

10. I have lost 10 passports.

Are We
There Yet?

Okay, kids, how many of you got what I was trying to do with the book title? (Hmmm, suddenly worried I've spent too much of the book talking like you're sitting opposite me. Sorry if that's been annoying – far too late in the day for me to go back and change it now – it's just really strange writing a book all on your tod when you're used to chatting AT people for a living. Anyway, I digress.)

Hopefully you'll remember, like I do, asking the question again and again on long journeys when you were sat in the back of the car, squeezed shoulder to shoulder with your siblings, empty Capri-Suns and Wotsit packets littering the footwells. After the umpteenth time of you repeating it, your mum turned around and said something like, 'If you don't stop arguing I'm going to crash the car!!!'

But as an adult, I think quite a few of us carry on asking the question, except the difference is we're now in the driving seat and it's no longer about reaching whichever family member's house we were heading to, it's about life. Have we made it yet? Are we doing what we want to do yet? Are we successful yet? Are we the happiest we'll ever be yet? Have we reached the know-the-answers-to-everything stage of adulthood yet?

I went into *I'm a Celeb* ... feeling sore and bruised. I was heartbroken over Jason and I wasn't where I wanted to be. I could see 30 looming on the horizon and it felt like I was in Tomb Raider, that PlayStation game where my friends would make Lara Croft swim but then drown her. I felt like I was in *Jurassic Park*, and the T-Rex (life) was coming for me with his small nasty hands and big teeth. It was exhausting.

After three weeks away from the real world, spending time with Nick Knowles (chilling in his hammock and knowing everything about everything), Anne Hegerty (who gave zero fucks) and John Barrowman (who made me silent scream-laugh in that Dolls House covered in spiders), and pushing myself to do things that would have scared the shit out of me a year before, I felt restored. I came out feeling like I'd had an epiphany: that everything was going to be okay in the end, that I still had everything left to play for and that I was enough, just as I was.

Now, having written this book, I don't think the jungle taught me that – I think I knew it all along; it was just that the jungle gave me the time and space to realise it. I've had some tough times in my life, but I've come out the stronger for it. I've been so lucky to have incredible people around me who have nurtured me, supported me, picked up the pieces when things have fallen apart and given me amazing opportunities. I've been utterly, utterly heartbroken, but I'm so happy I've been given this huge capacity to love. I've made a million mistakes along the way but I've also done things I'm so, so proud of. I can look at myself in the mirror, with or without my make-up on, and tell myself that I'm kind and generous and have things to share with the world. The jungle didn't make me strong; I was already strong because of everything that had happened before.

I'm not asking myself the question 'Am I there yet?' anymore. I'm no longer that kid sitting in the back of the car needing my mum to tell me that. I don't always feel like a fully functioning adult either, but then I'm not really sure anyone ever thinks that about themselves. What I am is a complicated, flawed human being with blonde hair, boobs and a brain, who wants to entertain people for as long as they're interested in letting me try.

The biggest lesson has been understanding that this mystical 'there' we're all aiming for isn't real. Maybe it comes from all the fairy tales we

grow up on, where there was always a conven-
ient happy ending that closed the story, usually
involving a prince and a big wedding. I'd still like
the big wedding, at Christmas, if that's okay, and
lots of babies would be great too. I just don't
want the 'ending' anymore. I'm more interested
in beginnings

When I started writing this book back in January
2019, I was sitting on a train heading to Manchester.
Considering it's now June, you'll be pleased to note
I did in fact reach Manchester and get off said train.
But, figuratively speaking, the 'journey' is still going.
People drop the word 'journey' a lot on tele, and
even though it sounds a bit wanky, I definitely think
I had one on *I'm a Celeb* ... and it was marvellous.
But it didn't stop at the end of the show. I'm still
on it now. In the last six months, I've made some
of the biggest and boldest choices about my career
and done things that have really petrified me, like
my stand-up tour, and I want to carry on doing
that. I want to keep pushing and finding out about
myself while being content with all that's happening
in the present, rather than aiming for some target
way off in the distance that I think is there but I
can't quite see.

I really hope that if you're feeling lost, whether

you're 19, 29 or 99, you're as lucky as I've been to have people around you who love you and will support you and provide you with the space you need to realise that you too are good enough, just as you are, and that tough times always pass in the end. Don't let other people's achievements sidetrack you and don't worry about the future. None of us are 'there yet'.

We are all exactly where we need to be.

About the Author

Emily Atack is an actress, comedienne, writer and TV host.

Best known for her role as Charlotte Hinchcliffe on award winning sit-com *The Inbetweeners* and as the 2018 runner up on *I'm A Celebrity . . . Get Me Out of Here*. Her debut stand up tour Talk Thirty To Me sold out across the UK.

Acknowledgements

Thank you to my editors Emily Barrett & Pippa Wright and the whole team at Seven Dials/Orion Publishing Group for this incredible opportunity. You have been the most amazing partners and I've loved working with you all.

My beautiful and talented parents Kate and Keith. You taught me to love and to always be kind. Be free, passionate and expressive. Your support knows no bounds and I couldn't have written this book without any of those things you have instilled in me.

My aunty Amy and uncle Bob. Your kitchen is the centre of my universe. Where all the ideas happen! Thank you for your endless love & support.

My cousin Lydia. Your strength, beauty and positivity blow my mind. You help me every single day, and encourage me to be the best version of myself I can be. An actual real life angel.

My agent Alex Segal. You gave me a shot when no one else would, you saw beneath what everyone else saw and gave me back my confidence in the business. A wonderful agent with my best interests at heart, and a true friend above all else.

My brother George. All round legend. Thanks for letting me steal most of your jokes.

My sister Martha. Without you I am nothing.